This book is a

Gift

From

....

To

....

Date

....

May God bless you through this book

QUEEN OF HEAVEN

QUEEN OF HEAVEN

PRAYER M. MADUEKE

PRAYER PUBLICATIONS
I Babatunde close, Off Olaitan Street,
Surulere, Lagos, Nigeria
+234 803 353 0599

QUEEN OF HEAVEN

Copyright © 2015

PRAYER M. MADUEKE

ISBN: 9781545024362

Prayer Publications

This book has been read and approved for publication by the General Overseer of the Mountain of Fire and Miracles Ministries, DR. D.K. OLUKOYA.

For further information or permission::

1 Babatunde close, off Olaitan Street, Surulere, Lagos, Nigeria
+234 803 353 0599
Email: pastor@prayermadueke.com,
Website: www.prayermadueke.com

TABLE OF CONTENTS

ACKNOWLEDGEMENTS

If not for God, writing this book would have been impossible. Therefore, it is proper that I begin by expressing my profound gratitude to the Lord Jesus who gave me the impetus to pick up my pen and begin to write at all about this principality. Glory be to His name in the highest.

I sincerely express my indebtedness to Dr. D. K. Olukoya, General Overseer of the Mountain of Fire and Miracles Ministries, who read the manuscript, sponsor and approved it for publication.

INTRODUCTION

The Queen of Heaven is one of the wicked and daring principalities that Satan trusts very much. She is connected with virtually all evil. She is to Satan whom the Holy Spirit is to God.

Her witchcraft is the most sophisticated in the list because she is in charge. She is the eternal partner of Satan. She is the direct executive of Satan.

No department of Satan's kingdom can act without her knowledge. She is in possession of every sinner's file. Satan himself, in most cases cannot do much without this principality. Her office is next to that of Satan. She is the inspirer of all false doctrines.

She is the overseer of dead churches and all evil groups, anti-God and anti-Christ organizations. She is the character builder of all evil men. Her chief ministry is to misinterpret, oppose and fight God and his people. Let us start:

Therefore, pray not thou for this people, neither lift up cry nor prayer for them, neither make intercession to me: for I will not hear thee. Seest thou not what they do in the cities of Judah and in the streets of Jerusalem?

The children gather wood, and the fathers kindle the fire, and the women knead their dough, to make cakes to the queen of heaven, and to pour out drink offerings unto other gods, that they may provoke me to anger. Jeremiah 7: 16-18

This is one of the few places in the scripture where God forbids prayers. In addition, for those who disobeyed God, went ahead, and prayed, God said He would not hear their prayers. Jeremiah is popularly known as the "weeping prophet". His tears always attracted divine intervention.

Chapter 1

QUEEN OF HEAVEN – WIFE OF SATAN

Whenever an individual or groups of individuals give their loyalty or co-operation to the Queen of Heaven, whether directly or indirectly. They become enemies of God. Moreover, unless the people turn to God in repentance, God will abandon them totally and destruction without remedy will become their lot. He (God) therefore commands that until they repent, no prayer should be offered, crying would not help the situation and intercession would fail. However, intercessors always fail in a situation like this.

REASONS WHY SOME PRAYERS ARE NOT ANSWERED

Seest thou not what they do in the cities of Judah and in the streets of Jerusalem? The children gather wood, and the fathers kindle the fire, and the women knead their dough, to make cakes to the queen of heaven, and to pour out drink offerings unto other gods, that they may provoke me to anger. Jeremiah 7: 17-18

God opened Jeremiah's eyes to see what people were doing in the cities. The sin of idolatry was committed right in the streets of Jerusalem by all members of every family. Cakes were made of honey, fine flour and other ingredients, were shapened like the moon to the replica of what the cakes were offered. They also practiced prostitution in connection with this worship. During the sacrifices, all the women-convert were to submit to immorality in identification with the god in this worship. This must be done at least once to perfect the offering. This, entry point demands immorality as a seal of covenant with the queen of heaven. Prophet Jeremiah confronted them concerning this and wanted them to go into repentance but they were determined to continue in their sin.

Moreover, thou shalt say unto them, thus saith the Lord; shall they fall, and not arise? Shall he turn away, and not return? Why then is this people of Jerusalem slidden back by a perpetual backsliding? They hold fast deceit, the refuse to return. I hearkened and heard, but they spake not aright: no man repented him of his wickedness, saying, what have I done? Everyone turned to his course, as the horse rusheth into the battle. Yea, the stork in the Heaven knoweth her appointed times; and the turtle and the crane and the swallow observe the time of their coming but my people know not the judgment of the Lord. How do ye say, we are wise, and the law of the Lord is with us? Lo, certainly in vain made he it; the pen of the Scribes is in vain. The wise men are ashamed, they are dismayed and taken: Lo, they have rejected the word of the Lord, and what wisdom is in them? Jeremiah 8: 4-9

The argument here is that when men fall, they get up again, and when they lose their ways, they turn and seek their way back home. However, a covenant with the Queen of Heaven makes people hold fast to the deceit. In the midst of their destruction, Jeremiah confessed the sins of Israel and pleaded that God should save them for the sake of His name.

O Lord, though our iniquities testify against us, do thou it. For thy name's sake: For our backslidings are many, we have sinned against thee. O the hope of Israel, the saviour thereof in time of trouble, why shouldest thou be as a stranger in the land, and as a wayfaring man that turneth aside to tarry for a night? Why shouldest thou be as a man astonied, as a mighty man that cannot save? Yet thou, O Lord, art in the midst of us, and we are called by thy name; leave us not. Jeremiah 14: 7-9

Nevertheless, God turned down the request as we can see in verses 10-12:

Thus saith the Lord unto this people. Thus have they loved to wander, they have not refrained their feet therefore the Lord doth not accept them; He will now remember iniquity, and visit their sins. Then said the Lord unto me, pray not for this people for their good. When they fast, I will not hear their cry; and when they offer burnt offering and oblation, I will not accept them; but I will consume them by the sword, by the famine, and by the pestilence.

The only solution is total repentance and turning away from the queen of heaven (- see the Book of Ezekiel 14: 12-21 and 15: 1). The Kingdom of the Queen of Heaven is a reality. It is a well-organized department in the satanic kingdom. It is a well-structured system assigned to exercise dominion over human life.

Chapter 2

UNMASKING THE QUEEN OF HEAVEN

It is pertinent to elaborate on the things {i.e. attitudes, behavior manifestation et cetera} that characterized the activities and personality of the wicked woman referred to as the Queen of Heaven.

1. **Wicked:**   The Queen of Heaven is morally corrupt and devilish. She is one of the fiercest vicious principalities in the kingdom of darkness. When her spirit is imparted into her victims, it makes them mischievous and often very roguish, though they may appear gentle. Her victims naturally live in vicious immorality. The Queen of Heaven causes her agents to be perfectly corrupt and full of faults. They are normally marked by violence, ferocity and aggressiveness. She is very destructive, harmful and always going beyond reasoning in her dealings with her victims. In terms of relationship, she is very dishonest.

2. **Dangerous:**   Unless you break covenant with the queen of heaven, she is very dangerous and can inflict people with the most harmful loss. A link with the queen of heaven brings uncertainty, lack, insecurity, instability and very precarious lifestyle. Such life is hanged in doubt as she exposes the victims to the risk of being

injured. She fights with the weapons of extreme fear, destroying the mind of her victims.

3. **Intelligent:** No matter your intelligence, her intelligence is of a very high degree compared with that of humans. Her mental capacity, thought energy, and power to marshal out evil can only be defeated with the knowledge of Christ.

4. **Masquerading/Hidden** (2Cor. 11: 14-15) Most of her actions and appearances, wear masks. She always pretends to be who she is not. She appears in mere disguise with something or personality to deceive the souls of men. She disguises to deceive the populace and many have embraced her, taking her to be a holy personality. She has many good names but underneath are many evil manifestations. She is very obscure and difficult to define, always dim, dark shrouded and far from reality.

5. **Stubborn:** She is very mulish, extremely and perversely unyielding. Once she has decided to kill, steal or destroy, she persists until she executes the mission. She is very persistent, resolute, and obstinate and difficulty to be persuaded against her will. She is very unreasonable, terribly evil and very stuborn with fake diplomacy. Once she starts an evil program, nobody can stop her, except God and those in covenant with God.

6. **Development:** The Queen of Heaven is the most developed, vast and scientifically in the kingdom of Satan. Her laboratory and technology cannot be equated with any in the world.

7. **Expository:** The queen of heaven makes her victims a public show. She removes privacy and makes a dings out of the victims life. She can turn the most respected personality into a public mockery and a case study to every manner of sickness and problems. She opens people's doors for problem to enter with ease.

The Queen of Heaven can convert her victims into highway for all kinds of evil transportation. She is the expositoriest to sin, disease and calamities.

8. **Dehumanizing:** This principality can turn a well-known respected gentle person into an animal like Nebuchadnezzar of Babylon.

She converts human qualities into a beast, leaving his natural use, burn in lust and filled in unrighteousness. She can change the truth into a lie and empower her victims to dishonor their own bodies with vile affections without feeling guilty. Once you are in covenant with her, she can disgrace you at will. In addition, no matter your position, she destroys without mercy, or without prior information.

Manifestations Of Queen Of Heaven In Various Countries

For the purpose of deceit, the Queen of Heaven answers different names in different places. When she established her kingdom in **Asia**, she appeared with the name Cybele. I met somebody in one of the Nigeria markets who introduced himself as somebody who sold Cybele products. On inquiry, I discovered that he did not know the meaning and origin of Cybele. Once you use Cybele products – like pomade, powder, perfume, etc; your dreams are likely to change.

When this principality visited **Babylon**, she answered another name, Ishtar. Once you receive any of her numerous names as a means of reaching God or as a mediator between you and God, a covenant has been established. Moreover, such a covenant needs to be broken in order to achieve your freedom from this wicked spirit.

She appeared to the people of **China**, and deceived them with the name Shing Moo.

In **Germany,** she deceived them with another name, **Virgin Hertha**. At **Etruscans**, she was known as Nutria, which means "Mother of God". The Queen of Heaven answered Indiani in **India**, while in **Ephesus** she was known as Diana. She appeared as a mother with a child in **Egypt** and was therefore, called Isis (mother, and Horus (child). To the entire Islamic world, she is called Allah. Moreover, to the Roman Catholic world, she is called Virgin Mary.

A particular religious organization believes that she answers forty-six thousand, two hundred and ninety-six petitions in a second. That is the reason they recite their Rosary as many times as they can. Truly, she answers prayers from the second heaven but that is what the scripture calls lying wonders.

Examples of such "answers" can be seen in the Exodus: Exodus 7: 10-13, 20-22; 8: 5-7, 20-23, 1Samuel 18: 10-11; 1 Thessalonians 2: 7-12; Revelation 16: 13-15, 13: 1-8 and 11-17.

Ministers of God in all generations have always warned people against this spirit of deceit and counterfeit. Anything God does is genuine, but Satan always brings a similitude of it, which invariably is a counterfeit. Every genuine thing God does, Satan brings along the counterfeit to deceive human beings and confuse those who desire to serve God. Somebody like Samson started very well but failed to finish well because of the activities of the Queen of Heaven in his life in the person of Delilah. To some of her victims, she empower them to forbid sex for power and effectiveness but must practice one or more doctrines that contradicts the scriptures, this is also a deceit. There are people like Samson today who try to exercise their spiritual gifts and power without realizing that the grace of God in their lives have departed or reduced because the Queen of Heaven has a hold in their lives.

In addition, she said, The Philistines be upon thee Samson. Moreover, he awoke out of his sleep, and said, I will go out as at other times before, and shake myself. In addition, he wits not that the Lord was departed from him. Judges 16: 20

When sin enters and becomes enthroned, all that would remain will be unprofitable (1Cor. 13: 1-3). Sin, such as unfaithfulness to the family, covetousness, jealousy, greed, anger, immorality, pride, and financial irresponsibility separates us from God's spirit who is the true source of biblical spiritual gifts.

What prevails today in some churches are:

1.   Miracles devoid of the mercy of God. (Luke. 9: 51-56)

2.   Healing 'power' without the holiness and righteousness of the Almighty God. (Mt. 7: 22-27, 23: 24-25, 7: 15-20, II Peter 2: 14-17; Micha 3:11).

3.   Power without righteousness and true doctrine (see the book) Acts 8: 9-13, 18-24.

4.   Faith divorced from other aspects of the fruit of the Holy Spirit 1 Cor. 13:2. Mat. 7: 20.

5.   Prosperity without the necessary purity within and without. Luke. 16: 13-19.

6.   Prophecies devoid of scriptural perceptions. There are some ministers, who rub things in their eyes to see; others wear big rings, while some swallow charms, etc. This is what is called in marine kingdom, "Triple" "S". (1). seeing without solutions. (2). Sanction for a season. (3). Sent on transfer. I will explain better in the pulpit. Jer. 23: 16-21, 25-27, 30-32.

7.   Abundance of gifts without the grace of our Lord Jesus Christ Mt. 7: 21 23, 1 Cor. 13: 1 –3.

8. Diverse kinds of tongues, yet without the biblical "bridled tongues" 1 Cor. 13: 1; James 11: 26, 3: 10 – 16.

9. Interpretation of tongues that lack divine inspiration Dan 5: 5, 6, 8, 25 – 30.

10. Claims of the gifts of discernment that is not accompanied by scriptural discipline Num. 22: 9 – 34.

11. Preaching of the word of God without practicing it James 1: 22 – 23.

12. Power to place a curse without power to bless. Some of them, their churches or denomination is a prison yard, an altar that is more difficult to leave than an occult group. The bound their members with fear. Many gatherings today are a gathering of witchcraft in the name of church. 1Kings 19:1 – 2

These are the activities of the Queen of Heaven in the body of Christ in the last day. In many passages of the Bible, we are warned that in the last day, there will be an unprecedented explosion of falsehood teachings throughout the world.

We are of God: he that knoweth God heareth us: he that is not of God heareth us not. Hereby know we the spirit of truth, and the spirit of error. 1Jn. 4: 6

However, there are still genuine, life-saving, pure miracles and churches from God through the operation of the gifts of the Holy Spirit. Nevertheless, the emphasis here is that we must be able to identify the lying wonders of the Queen of Heaven, which she performs through her agents.

Chapter 3

IDENTIFYING WORSHIPPERS OF
THE QUEEN OF HEAVEN

The desire of the queen of heaven is to capture the whole reverence or worship meant for God under heaven. She demands full worship from all creatures and where she fails to receive direct worship, she presents a false identity in the similitude of God under the auspices of religion through which men and women will eventually worship her. In addition, once you accept such an identity, your worship and all you do will be diverted to the Queen of Heaven. The purpose of the false identity is to defile and pollute human worship. Nevertheless, there is a divine warning in the book of Isaiah.

To the law and testimony: if they speak not according to this word. It is because there is no limit in them. Isaiah 8: 20

Any name put between God and humans except that of Christ is from the Queen of Heaven.

For there is one God, and one mediator between God and men, the man Christ Jesus (1 Timothy 2:5).

In terms of communicating with God by prayer, worship and songs, Christ is the ultimate. Both the Old and New Testaments agree and warn the people of every generation against attaching any other name to Christ in terms of worship or prayer to God (see Deuteronomy).

The Lord thy God will raise up unto thee a prophet from the midst of thee, they of thy brethren, like unto me: unto him, ye shall hearken. Here, Moses referred the people to Christ.

I will raise them up a Prophet from among their brethren, like unto thee, and will put my words in his mouth: and he shall speak unto them all that I shall command him.

And it shall come to pass, that whosoever will not hearken unto my words which he shall speak in my name, I will require it of him (Deut. 18: 15, 18-19). Moses, a recognized authority, both in the old and the New Testament referred us to Christ.

When Isaiah was tired of human complaints, he consoled them with divine revelation and assured them that God was coming up with a deliverer.

Therefore the Lord himself shall give you a sign; Behold, a virgin shall conceive and bear a son, and shall call his name Immanuel (Isaiah 7: 14). See also Isaiah 9: 6.

All the prophets were pointing to Christ as none of them claimed to have solutions to human problems before Christ was born, many false prophets had come and deceived many, as can be seen in Acts of the apostles.

Then stood there up one in the council, a Pharisee, named Gamaliel, a doctor of the law, had in reputation among all the people, and commanded to put the apostles forth a little space; And said unto them, ye men of Israel take heed to yourselves what ye intend to do as touching these men; For before these days ruse up Theudas, boasting himself to be some body to whom a number of men, about four hundred, joined themselves: who was slain; and all, as many as obeyed were scattered, and brought to naught. After this man rose up Judas of Galilee in the days of the taxing, and all, even as many as obeyed him, were dispersed. Acts 5: 34 – 37:

Multitudes and the leaders of the day were confused as to whether Christ was from God or not. The people of God were divided and none of the group could persuade the other. At that point, God intervened and spoke in the hearing of all.

While he yet spake, behold, a bright cloud overshadowed them: and behold a voice out of the cloud, which said, this is my beloved Son, in whom I am well pleased, hear ye him. Matt 17:5

And there was a cloud that overshadowed them; and a voice came out of the cloud, saying, "This is my beloved Son: hear Him". Mark 9:7. If you doubt Moses and Elijah will you also doubt God?

The next day John seeth Jesus coming unto him, and saith, Behold the Lamb of God, which taketh away the sin of the world. Again the next day after John stood, and two of his disciples; And looking upon Jesus as he walked, he saith, Behold the Lamb of God! And the two disciples heard him speak, and they followed Jesus. Philip findeth Nathanael, and saith unto him, we have found him, of whom Moses in the law, and the prophets, did write, Jesus of Nazareth, the son of Joseph. John 1:29, 35-37, 45. John said here; this is the last sacrifice provided by God Himself, a perfect sacrifice.

John the Baptist directed people to Christ. He separated himself and presented Christ. When the apostles wrought a miracle by healing the lame at the beautiful gate, people wanted to focus on them but Peter rejected it and said:

Neither is there salvation in any other: for there is none other name under Heaven given among men, whereby we must be saved (Acts 4: 12).

When John the beloved was about to worship at the feet of an angel, the angel restrained him (Revelation 22: 8 – 9). In one of Jesus' preaching's, He was teaching about the Queen of Heaven, unclean spirits and a woman who was possessed by the spirit of the Queen of Heaven interrupted Him and tried to divert and confuse the mind of the simple. Jesus stopped her and prevented her from directing attention of true worshippers to mere mortals, womb that bore him or paps that He sucked.

And it came to pass, as he spake these things, a certain woman of the company lifted up her voice, and said unto him, Blessed is the womb that bore thee, and the paps which thou has sucked (Luke 11: 27).

Nevertheless, Jesus rebuked her and rejected her teaching (Verse 28).

However, he said, yea rather, blessed are they that hear the word of God, and keep it.

This evil personality in the days of Mary wanted to divert people's attention to the name Mary, but Jesus said that those who would receive blessings were those who heard the word of God and did it. (Luke 11: 28). However, what is the word of God?

WHAT IS THE WORD OF GOD?

The word of God is what Paul said in 1 Timothy 2: 5:

For there is one God, and one mediator between God and men, the man Christ Jesus.

It is what Moses said in Deuteronomy 18: 15, 18:

The Lord thy God will raise up unto thee a prophet from the midst of thee, of thy brethren, like unto me; unto him ye shall hearken; I will raise them up a prophet from among their brethren, like unto thee, and will put my words in his mouth; and he shall speak unto them all that I shall command him.

It is what Isaiah said in Isaiah 7: 14. 9: 6:

Therefore the Lord himself shall give you a sign: Behold a virgin shall conceive, and hear a son, and shall call his name Immanuel: For unto us a child is born, unto us a son is given, and the government shall be upon his shoulders; and his name shall be called Wonderful Counselor, the Mighty God, The Everlasting Father, The Prince of Peace.

The word of God is what God Himself said in Matthew 17: 3-5. 3: 17:

And, behold there appeared unto Moses, and Elias talking with him. Then answered Peter and said unto Jesus, Lord it is good for us to be here: if thou wilt let us make here three tabernacles, one for thee, and one for Moses, and for Elias. While he yet space, behold, a bright cloud overshadowed them: and behold a voice out of the cloud, which said, this is my beloved son, in whom I am well pleased, hear ye him.

The word of God is what John the Baptist said in John 1: 29, 35 – 37, and verse 45:

The next day John seeth Jesus coming unto him and saith, Behold the Lamb of God which taketh away the sin of the world. And again, the next day after John stood, and two of his disciples; And looking upon Jesus as he walked, he said, Behold the Lamb of God! And the two disciples heard him speak, and they followed Jesus.

Philip findeth Nathaniel, and saith unto him, we have found him, of whom Moses in the Law, and the prophets, did write, Jesus of Nazareth, the son of Joseph.

The word of God is what the angels of God said in Revelation 22: 8 – 9:

And I John saw these things, and heard them. And when I had seen, I fell down to worship before the feet of the angel, which showed me these things.

Then saith he unto me, see thou do it not: for I am thy fellow servant, and of thy brethren and prophets, and of them, which keep the sayings of this book: worship God.

The word of God is what the Virgin Mary said in John 2: 5, 7:

His mother saith unto the servants, whatsoever he saith unto you, do it. Jesus saith unto them; fill the water pots with water. And they filled them up to the brim.

It is like saying, do not ever come back to me and they never went back to her. WHAT IS THE WORD OF GOD?

It is what the scriptures say in Philippians 2: 9 – 10:

Wherefore God also hath highly exalted him and given him a name, which is above every name: That at the name of Jesus every knee should bow, of things in Heaven and things in earth and things under the earth.

It is what Christ Himself said in John 14: 6:

Jesus, saith unto him, I am the way, the truth and the life: no man cometh unto the Father, buy by me.

Jesus is the only way. His mother, his disciples etc are not the way and that was why they directed true followers to Christ. They know and believe that one day they will die and will no longer be available on earth to pray for us even if they wish, why? They are not omnipotent or Omnipresent, they can only be in heaven or on earth and if in heaven, they can no longer help us, pray for us or assist us in any way. So, knowing that the Queen of heaven may appear with their names to deceive people, the directed us to Christ who only is Omnipresent.

In addition, Matthew 11: 28 say:

Come unto me all ye that labour and are heavy laden and I will give you rest.

Paul said that we are complete in Him (Christ) – Col. 2: 9 – 10:

For in him dwelleth all the fullness of the Godhead bodily. Moreover, ye are complete in him, which is the head of all principality and power.

When you have Jesus, you do not need any other person, especial the dead to pray for you, even the saint, otherwise you will be practicing necromancy. With Him, you can stand-alone and still win any battle like the three Hebrew children, shedrack, Meshach and Abednego and also; like Daniel in the lion's den and like Joseph in Potiphar's house and in prison. When you are sure of divine support, you can stand and get victory like Elijah against all the prophets. When you are sure of Christ, Pharaoh will bow; Nebuchadnezzar will confess that there is no other God except the Almighty God, your own God (Daniel 3: 24 – 30). Darius will reverse the decree, Lazarus will be brought to life, you will have a life partner, not a life enemy as wife or husband, and impossibilities will be made possible. Hannah will sing:

He will keep the feet of His saints, and the wicked shall be silent in darkness; for by strength shall no man prevail. The adversaries of the Lord shall be broken to pieces; out of heaven shall He thunder upon them: the Lord shall judge the ends of the earth; and he shall give strength unto his king, and exalt the horn of his anointed (1 Samuel 2: 9 10).

Once the presence of Jesus Christ is with you, barrenness will tremble, kingdoms will shake, your Goliath will die; and you will not need the support of any dead saint or the approval of any living saints. After all, who are the saints? They are those who died in Christ and those who are living in Christ. For the living saint in Christ Jesus, the militant church, we can pray for one another. No dead soldier can fight again. We who are alive in Christ should fight our battles.

Now therefore ye are no more strangers and foreigners, but fellow citizens with the saints, and of the household of God; and are built upon the foundation of the apostles and prophets, Jesus Christ himself being the chief corner stone; That at that time ye were without Christ, being aliens from the commonwealth of Israel, and strangers from the covenants of promise, having no hope and without God in the world: but now in Christ Jesus ye who sometimes were far off are made nigh by the blood of Christ. Eph. 2: 19 – 20; 12-13

We are fellow citizens with the dead saints, not strangers or foreigners. We can do even much more than they did. We have greater privilege (James 5: 17 –18). Elijah was a man subject to like passions as we are, and he prayed earnestly that it might not rain; and it rained not on the earth by the space of three years and six months. In addition, he prayed again, heaven gave rain, and the earth brought forth her fruits. No Christian has any justifiable excuse or reason to fail in life.

Jesus said unto him, if thou canst believe, all things are possible to him that believeth (Mark 9: 23).

If the queen of heaven discovers that you are religious and insist on serving God, she will try to give you a name and once you accept that, she can even give you some gifts (power) to perform false miracles, the triple "S" or lying wonders. The children of Israel were deceived for seventy years before they discovered that they were not serving the true God.

Then came the word of the Lord of hosts unto me, saying, speak unto all the people of the land, and to the priests, saying, when ye fasted and mourned in the fifth and seventh months, even those seventy years, did ye all fast unto me, even to me? Moreover, when ye did eat, and when ye did drink, did not ye eat and when ye did drink, did not ye eat for yourselves? Zechariah 7: 46

The Samaritan woman at the well confessed that since she was born, she belonged to a family, a church denomination or religious group that was worshipping God in a particular place but surprisingly, when she saw the person she thought she had been worshipping, she could not recognize Him. Supposing she was fifty years old at the time of meeting Christ, when she saw Jesus, she was disappointed by the Lord's statement. I pray it will not be our portion, in the mighty name of Jesus.

Ye worship ye know not what: we know what we worship: for salvation is of the Jews. The woman saith unto him, I know that Messias cometh, which is called Christ: when he is come, he will tell us all things. Jesus saith unto her, I that speak unto thee am he. John 4: 22, 25, 26

The woman saith unto him, I know that Messias cometh, which is called Christ: when he is come, he will tell us all things. Jesus saith unto her, I that speak unto thee am he.

It is therefore possible to worship God sincerely with all your heart contrary to the scriptures only to end up in hell fire. It will not be wise to drop this book, label it anti what you strongly believed in. Check your believe, search the scriptures and see if you are sincerely wrong and take decision while it is yet not late.

Many people, who worship without reference to the scriptures, will be disappointed on the last day. Crowns are exchangeable, so take heed least another takes your own (Matthew 7: 21-23).

Chapter 4

QUEEN OF HEAVEN – AN ANCIENT OBJECT OF WORSHIP

Gwen Shaw in his book "Redeeming the Land" gives details of the queen of heaven as an ancient worship. The worship of false gods under the influence of the queen of heaven with different names began long time ago. As the population of the world grew in those days, the iniquity of men waxed stronger on a continual basis until the earth was fully corrupt, destroyed, and brought to ruin.

Pulling down, wounding, killing of individuals and the entire cities became an order of the day, just like what we are witnessing today in many nations. There was perversion, wickedness, violence, and unrighteous gain {i.e. greed, the spirit of greed) everywhere. Genesis 6: 1-7. However, in the midst of these, God found only one righteous man, Noah (Genesis 6: 8 –10, 13). The wicked people in the world were then destroyed in a terrible flood. This took place 1,656 years after God had created Adam. God then started a new world family with Noah.

The three sons of Noah were Shem, Japheth and Ham.

Shem: Gen.5:32. 1 Chron. 1: 17 – 34, from these above passages you can see that Shem was the

35

father of the Shemities, e.g. Abraham, Ishmael, Isaac, Esau and Israel.

Japheth: 1 Chronicles 1: 5 – Japhet means encouragement or extension (1 Chron. 11: 5-6) from which came the nations of Northern Europe, Germans, French, Welsh, Irish, Britons and many other Anglo-Saxon races. (Magog 1 Chron. 1: 5, Russia, Ezk. 38: 2, 39: 6; Rev. 20: 8). In fact, from Japheth you get Medes, Persians, Greeks, Italians, Portuguese and other nationalities.

Ham: 1Chron. 1: 8-10; Isaiah 1: 11. From this cursed Ham you get Egypt, Arabia, Babylon, India, Libyans and other tribes in North Africa (Ezk. 27: 10, 30: 5; Isaiah 46: 9). When Noah became very old, the spirit of the Queen of Heaven influenced him into drunkenness. The same spirit entered into Ham to look upon his father's nakedness. The same spirit caused Noah to curse his son Ham (Gen. 9: 18-25).

From this cursed family, Cush was born. His descendants dwelt from Ethiopia to Euphrates. Cush was the founder of Nineveh, Babylon and other cities in the Arab nations (Gen. 10: 7).

Cush: was known as a ringleader in the great Apostasy. He contributed greatly in leading humankind away from the worship of the true God. He was called *Bel* (the co-founder). He founded Babylon (Ger. 50: 2). He was the original prophet of idolatry and the author of pagan rites.

He was the father of Nimrod called Ninus. He became the "father of gods". In Egypt, he was called *Hermes*, i.e. "the son of Ham". Cush the son of Ham, set about to free himself and the people who followed him from the laws of God and His righteousness. Hence, he became the first great leader of Apostasy while his son Nimrod was lifted up as the "Apostate Emancipator and Liberator" of humans. In the same way, Thaddaeus and Judas "liberated" Israel. People are easily deceived and brainwashed, be warned (Genesis 11: 1 – 9). He sought solutions outside God. He wanted to live independently and as a result, diverted from God (see 1Kings 12: 25 – 33).

The Spirit of the Queen of Heaven in Nimrod

And Cush begat Nimrod; he began to be a mighty one in the earth. He was a mighty hunter before the Lord: Wherefore it is said, Even as Nimrod the mighty hunter before the LORD. And the beginning of his kingdom was Babel, and Erech, and Accad and Calneh, in the land of Shinar Out of that land went forth Asshur, and builded Nineveh, and the city Rehoboth, and Calah, and Resen between Nineveh and Calah: the same is a great city. Genesis 10: 8 – 12

It is evident that all pagan religions have their beginning in Babylon under the rebellious and powerful descendants of Ham, through his son Cush and grandson Nimrod. There is no one good thing to be said about Nimrod. Cush was evil. Nevertheless, Nimrod, the son of Cush, was many times more evil. Nimrod has many evils associated with him. The name Nimrod means, "Rebel, obstinate, indignant, conqueror of the leopard". He was called a mighty hunter. The Jewish Encyclopedia says, "Nimrod was he who made all people rebellious against God. He compelled the people to worship him as a deity. Therefore, he became the first anti-Christ. He was the first deified mortal. He subdued his neighbours by an occasion of forces and overcame all the people of the east. He was the first to invent magic acts and the motions of the stars. He was of a war-like disposition, ambitious for glory and he was the first to carry out war against his neighbours. He conquered all nations from Assyria to Libya. He was worshipped as god like Nebuchadnezzar, Alexander the Great, the Neros; even Napoleon and Hitler who believed themselves to be invincible". Hence, some names have been associated with the name of Nimrod. They include:

The Horned one, Winged Bull, Nimrod, the Centaur, the fabulous half-horse, half-man; the father of gods. Nimrod was worshipped in many nations with many different names.

The spirit of the queen of heaven comes in many forms. It always modifies herself to suit the customs and cultures of the people whom she wants to deceive. Nimrod was called the emancipator or deliverer, the mansion-connected with freemasonry. He was a bold man and of great strength. He persuaded men not to ascribe their strength to God; rather he persuaded them to believe that it was their own courage, which procured whatever happiness they achieve in life. He told people to fight and revenge on God for destroying their ancestors with flood. He pretended to love them (1 Kings 12: 25 – 33).

And the whole earth was of one language, and of one speech. And it came to pass, as they journeyed from the east, that they found a plain in the land of Shinar, and they dwelt there. And they said one to another, Go to, let us make brick, and burn them thoroughly, and they had brick for stones, and slime had they for mortar. And they said, Go to, let us build us a city and a tower, whose top may reach unto heaven; and let us make us a name, lest we he scattered abroad upon the face of the whole earth. And the LORD came down to see the city and the tower, which the children of men builded. And the LORD said, Behold, the people is one, and they have all one language: and this they begin to do and now nothing will be restrained from them, which they have imagined to. Go to, let us go down, and there confound their language, that they may not understand one another's speech. So the LORD scattered them abroad from thence upon the face of all the earth: and they left off building the city. Therefore is the name of it called Babel: because the LORD did there confound the language of all the earth; and from thence did the LORD scatter them abroad upon the face of all the earth. Genesis 11: 1 – 9

He deemed it a sign of cowardice to submit to God; thus, they built a tower that the flood would not get to. The place wherein they built the tower was called Babylon because of the confusion of the language. Babel stands for confusion.

Spirit of the Queen of Heaven in Semiramis

He said also unto me, turn thee yet again and thou shalt see greater abominations that they do. Then he brought me to the door of the gate of the Lord's house, which was toward the north: and, behold, there sat women weeping for Tammuz. Ezekiel 8: 13-14

Tammuz was the Babylonian god of spring; He was the husband or lover of the goddess Ishtar. There was serious mourning when Nimrod's life was suddenly terminated. Much hardship followed his death. People were left without a deliverer. Semiramis, the wife of Nimrod, pregnant at that time gave birth to a baby boy. With her powerful witchcraft manipulations, she convinced the people that her husband, Nimrod, had risen from the dead. She did this in fulfilling Genesis 3: 15.

And I will put enmity between thee and the woman, and between thy seed and her seed; it shall bruise they head, and thou shall bruise thy head, and thou shalt bruise his heel

That is, the spirit that introduced the honor and worship of "mother and son". The worship of Nimrod soon spread all over the world with Queen of Heaven given it different names.

Eventually, the worship was shifted to Semiramis and her husband/son.The worshippers believed that worshipping him brought life to their farms and vegetation. They believed that as long as they wept before his altar he would arise from the dead and bless them.

Chapter 5

THE QUEEN OF HEAVEN WAS BEING WORSHIPPED IN DIFFERENT NATIONS WITH THE FOLLOWING NAMES

Athens - Cybil, **Egypt -** Isis/Horus or Osiris

China - Shengmu or Shing Moo –, which means Holy mother

Scandinavia – Disa, pagan **Rome,** Fortuna and the boy Jupiter, **Greece –** Ceres, means the great mother with a baby on her breasts or as Irene the goddess of peace with the boy Plutus in her arms. The ancient belief was that the curse could only be removed from the earth by the great "deliverer" or an "emancipator". Many religions in many nations believed some deceivers in the past, including Horus of Egypt, Krishna of India, and Thor of Scandinavia. All were worshipped as gods, who had crushed the serpent or killed the serpent to free people from the power of the devil over him (Genesis 3: 15). In Acts, chapter 19, she was being worshiped at Ephesus as Diana. Her temple was one of the "seven wonders of the world". It was 425 feet by 220 feet, and had 127 columns of marble, each 60 feet high. Women and eunuchs performed services at the temple services. After performing the rites, the temple prostitutes would appear and offer their bodies as acts of sacrifice to the devotees.

To perfect the worship of Diana, immorality had to be practiced in the temple. In Ephesus, in 431 Ad at the Council of the Ephesus, the Church Fathers condoned the worship of Mary, and it became an official doctrine of the church at this council. The Israelites worshipped the queen of heaven in Judges 2: 13, 10: 6. This was the spirit that destroyed Solomon (see 1 Kings 11: 1 – 6; 11 Kings 23: 13, 17: 41; Acts 19: 27). King Solomon married seven hundred wives – princesses – and had three hundred concubines. With these women around him his children must have been counted into thousands if all these had children for him, yet when he died none of his children was found responsible enough to occupy the throne. The "small boy", Rehoboam, could not even answer a common question and his response divided the kingdom. Such is the work of the queen of heaven

The Goddess of Occultism

The queen of heaven feeds on blood and she is responsible for all the secret societies in the world. She is in charge of sorcery, magic, witchcraft, divination and idolatry. She gives power to native doctors, herbalists, etc. She also gives wealth, protection, fame, health, children and life (all her gifts are fake and temporary). These are the things she claims to offer people under her.

And he had power to give life unto the image of the beast, that the image of the beast should both speak and cause that as many as would not worship the image of the beast should be killed. Revelation 13:15

She is in charge of raising or promoting a person for her selfish use and at the peak of power, dumps the person, thus making a caricature of such a man or woman.

Queen of Heaven – Great Prostitute

And there came one of the seven angels which had the seven veils, and talked with me, saying unto me, come hither; I will show unto thee the judgment of the great whore that sitteth upon many waters. Revelation 17:1

The description "great whore" or "prostitute" talks about her communication network system. It is a religious power that is in charge of controlling all religious groups worldwide. She sitteth (present tense), means that she had been in operation, is still in operation and will continue until the day of her judgment. "Many waters," as used in that portion of the scripture represents all parts of the world. The queen of heaven is the sole administrator of the satanic government; her kingdom is worldwide. Water in the scriptural interpretation represents the world, sea of humanity.

Queen of Heaven in Alliance with Rulers of Nations

With whom the kings of the earth have committed fornication, and the inhabitants of the earth have been made drunk with the wine of her fornication. Revelations 17: 2

The influence of the queen of heaven is on almost every throne and on every governmental set-up, since the creation of the world. She, in corroboration with Satan was the personality that was used as a serpent to overthrow our first parents Adam and Eve (Genesis 3: 1-7). Committing fornication with kings of the earth means having an unholy relationship with kings. Any support given to God's enemy in act of sin is likened to committing fornication. She compelled kings to pass evil decrees into law. She influences kings and government authorities to enact laws contrary to God's will. She motivated the three presidents who worked with Daniel to a law that contradicted the belief of Daniel so that Daniel's destiny could be terminated. She stirred Nebuchadnezzar to build an image so that worship would be directed to her through image worship (see Daniel 3: 1 – 7). Anybody who places an image, object or a statue of anything to worship God is not worshipping Christ but the queen of heaven (Exodus 20: 5). In the book of Esther, her target was Mordecai and the Jews. Shadrach Meshach and Abednego were never left in her evil scheme of influencing authority to rid men's destiny.

The queen of heaven uses kings and people in authority to draw the inhabitants of the earth to make people get drunk in the worship of the queen of heaven. They teach more and practice little.

Woe unto you scribes and Pharisees, hypocrites! For ye devour widows' houses, and for pretence make a long prayer: therefore ye shall receive the greater damnation. Woe unto you, scribes and Pharisees hypocrites! For ye compass sea and land to make one proselyte, and when he is made, ye make him twofold, more the child of hell than yourselves (Matthew 23: 14 – 15).

The proselytes were not Jews but dwelt in Israel. They were uncircumcised but were thought to observe Jewish laws. They were called the scabs of the Jewish church. History records that they were bitterer against Christ and Christians than the Jews (Revelations 17: 2) were. Her (queen of heaven's) aim was to get to the top where she could stay to control the inhabitants of the earth and make them do more evil than the king: "Old people declared war but the young ones are "fighting the war" (Ezekiel 14: 12 – 21). The queen of heaven is the goddess of evil and inspiration behind indecent dressing (Revelation 17: 3). She is in charge of tailors and fashion designers who sew seductive dresses for women. She also oversees the practice of women putting on clothes strictly for men and vice-versa (Deuteronomy 22: 5; Ezekiel 13: 17-19, 22; Jeremiah 40: 30; 2 Kings 9: 30).

Queen of Heaven, the Goddess of Evil Names

So he carried me away in the spirit into the wilderness: and I saw a woman sit upon a scarlet colored beast, full of names of blasphemy, having seven heads and ten horns. Revelation 17: 3

No matter how close a name is to God, once the queen of heaven offers it, it should be rejected. She has used the names of good people who served God to fight against God and His people. The scripture calls any name from the queen of heaven names of blasphemy. Once you receive it, all your worship, prayers and activities are blaspheming to God.

See also Proverbs 18: 10.

The name of the Lord is a strong tower: the righteous runneth into it, and is safe.

1 Timothy 2: 5 says:

For there is one God, and one mediator between God and men, the man Christ Jesus.

Only the blessed Holy Trinity is omnipresent, as such they are everywhere and in every situation.

Revelation 1: 18:

I am he that liveth, and was dead; and, behold I am alive for evermore, Amen; and have the keys of hell and of death

According to Acts 4: 12:

48

Neither is there salvation in any other: for there is none other name under heaven given among men, whereby we must be saved.

Any other name you are using in communicating with God in prayer is a deceit. We can call God the God of Abraham, Isaac and Jacob even the God of Mary but none of the names should be used with regard to prayer. Otherwise, you will be blaspheming against God. Once you use a name in prayer other than the name of God, no matter how holy the name may seem; it amounts to worshiping idols. Even if you receive an answer to prayer, say in the blasphemous name, it is a response from the queen of heaven.

And he doeth great wonders, so that he maketh fire come down from heaven on the earth in the sight of men. And deceiveth them that dwell on the earth by the means of those miracles, which he had power to do in the sight of the beast; saying to them that dwell on the earth, that they should make an image to the beast, which had the wound by a sword, and did live. And he had power to give life unto the image of the beast, that the image of the beast should be killed. Revelation 13: 13 – 15

Queen of Heaven, the Goddess of Money

And the woman was arrayed in purple and scarlet colours, and decked with gold and precious stones and pearls, having a golden cup in her hand full of abominations and filthiness of her fornication. Revelation 17: 4

The "gold" represents money and all that money can buy, people do everything just to get money.

Queen of Heaven, the Goddess of Abominations

And the woman was arrayed in purple and scarlet colures and decked with gold and precious stones and pearls, having a golden cup in her hand full of abominations and filthiness of her fornication. And upon her forehead was a name written. MYSTERY, BABYLON THE GREAT, THE MOTHER OF HARLOTS AND ABOMINATIONS OF THE EARTH. Revelation 17: 4 –5

The golden cup in her hand signifies that she is in possession of all the needs of men but to get anything through her, you have to commit abomination and do filthy things. Evil covenants and curses are attached to her. If people tell you how they make money through entry into secret societies, you will be greatly marveled and shocked. The cup is attractive outside but full of abominations inside. You cannot get any free gift from the queen of heaven. You must commit abomination. This verse says that all the past, present and future abominations must come from this evil woman, the queen of heaven. She is the mother of HARLOTS AND ABOMINATIONS OF THE EARTH, {past, present and future}. Therefore, if you or anybody is committing abomination, you are an instrument in the hands of the queen of heaven in giving birth to it.

Queen of Heaven, the Goddess of States War, Violence and Deaths

Revelation 17: 6 says:

And I saw the woman drunken with the blood of the saints, and with the blood of the martyr's of Jesus: and when I saw her, I wondered with great admiration.

In her quest for more blood, the queen of heaven gives names to different people, supplies them with weapons of war. She causes wars and supplies weapons of mass destruction. She loses nothing when she kills two groups of people that are faithful to her, because she still takes them to hell fire. She kills people and drinks their blood. She feeds on human blood to become stronger. She is anti-peace. She gives inspiration to his faithful to invent weapons of war. She does not go to the battlefield, but these weapons do battle for her. Billions of demons and human agents are working for the kingdom of this queen of heaven through invention of lethargy weapons. She has never appeared in the battlefield, yet she has killed more than all the greatest warriors put together. Her computer is the most sophisticated. Her own satellite is in the second heaven from where she monitors the whole earth. Unless you fight her from the heavenlies, you will not be able to do much to her kingdom (Ephesians 2: 6).

The queen of heaven drinks the blood of saints. There are two groups of saints. The living saints and the dead saints. The queen of heaven has imprisoned some of the saints, and placed an embargo on the promises and plans of God for their lives. She has eaten them alive and killed their destinies, like Lazarus the beggar

And there was a certain beggar named Lazarus, which was laid at his gate, full of sores. And desiring to be fed with the crumbs, which fell from the rich man's table: the dogs came and licked his sores. And it came to pass, that the beggar died, and was carried by the angels into Abraham's bosom. The rich man also died, and was buried. Luke 16: 20 – 22

He did not claim the promises of God before he died, yet when he got to heaven, he was without mansion. Even in heaven, Lazarus was still dwelling under Abraham. If not for God and Abraham's argument, the rich man would have persuaded Lazarus to serve him even though the rich man was in hell and Lazarus was in heaven. I refuse to go to heaven like Lazarus I want to go to heaven like Enoch, Abraham, Elijah, John the beloved etc. God forbid that I will not have a place in heaven. The bosom of Abraham will not be my portion. The angel of the Lord will take me to a place as good as Abraham's mansion or better than his because I have a better opportunity (Ephesians 2: 19-20).

And from the days of John the Baptist until now the kingdom of Heaven suffereth violence, and the violent take it by force. Matthew 11: 12

The only language the queen of heaven understands is war, violence, open enmity and direct confrontation (Luke 15: 25 – 31, Psalm 24: 1). If a man is poor, he should not blame God, rather, he should search within him and situation of his destiny. He has provided everything that we need (Nahum 3: 1 – 4).

The second group of living saints is those who know their rights and insist on getting them. They are the militant Christian soldiers of Christ. What shall we then say to these things? If God be for us, who can be against us? He that spared not his own son, but delivered him up for us all, how shall he not with him also freely give us all things? (Romans 8: 31–32).

They are the determined warriors ready to fight to the end (Romans 8: 38 – 39). They are those who are ready to fight to the last hour (11 Samuel 23:10). The other group of saints are those who refused Satan's helping hand (Hebrews 11: 35 – 38, Revelation 17: 6). They were the martyrs of Jesus, men who remained faithful unto the end (Revelation 6: 9-11).

The Interpretation of Water

And he saith unto me, the waters which thou sawest, where the whore sitteth, are peoples, and multitudes, and nations, and tongues. **Rev. 17: 15**

This woman has gone through the whole world with false religions. She has gone to every group of people, multitudes, nations and tongues. Even today, she is still sitting on many people's lives; controlling; nations and tongues (Acts 8: 5-8). She sits on people's marriages, businesses, academic work and many other aspects of human life. The queen of heaven is a thief. However, you can unseat her today.

Then all the men which knew that their wives had burned incense unto other gods, and all the women that stood by, a great multitude, even all the people that dwelt in the land of Egypt, in Pathros, answered Jeremiah, saying as for the word that thou hast spoken unto us in the name of the Lord, we will not hearken unto thee. But we will certainly do whatsoever things goeth forth out of our own mouth, to burn incense unto the queen of heaven, and to pour out drink offerings unto her, as we have done, we and our fathers, our kings and our princes, in the cities of Judah, and in the streets, of Jerusalem: for then had we plenty of victuals and were well, and saw no evil. But since we left off to burn incense to the queen of heaven, and to pour out the drink offerings unto her, we have wanted all things, and have been consumed by the sward and by the famine. (Jeremiah 44: 15-18)

Any little cooperation or sacrifice to the queen of heaven attracts a covenant and you must pay for that. When the people of Israel tried to stop worshipping her, they could not, because of the covenant made with her by their fathers. No, they tried to serve God after making a vow to the queen of heaven (see Jeremiah 44: 25, 17). Any little vow to the queen of heaven must be performed for the rest of one's life unless one is determined to fight her with the name of the Lord. The queen of heaven is wicked and ticklish. You cannot make profit from her kingdom and pay your tithe to God. Nobody can serve two masters at the same time. She was the goddess at the River Nile that supplied abundance to the Egyptians for seven years, and emptied the whole thing for another seven years.

When you see sinners prospering without Christ, do not envy them. You need the spirit of God and the wisdom of Joseph to overcome the evil days. Everybody is going to pay much more than he or she has benefited from the queen of heaven. Today, you see servants riding on horses and princes walking on their bare foot. That cocaine pushers are making it does not make what they do right before God. You do not have to envy them. They will soon vomit all those things. Even those faithful worshippers of the queen of heaven in Joseph's days, were also punished by the queen when the famine began.

And Joseph said, Give your cattle; and I will give you for your cattle, if money fail. And they brought their cattle unto Joseph; and Joseph gave them bread in exchange for horses, and for the flocks, and for the cattle of the herds, and for the asses; and he fed them with bread for all their cattle for that year, when that year was ended, they came unto him the second year, and said unto him, we will not hide it from my lord, how that our money is spent; my lord also hath our herds of cattle; there is not ought left in the sight of my lord, but our bodies, and our land; wherefore shall we die before thine eyes, both we and our land? Buy us and our land for bread, and our land and we will be servants unto Pharaoh; and give us seed, that we may live, and not die, that the land be not desolate. And Joseph bought all the land of Egyptians sold every man his field, because the famine prevailed over them; so the land became Pharaoh's. Genesis 47: 16-20

Joseph fought the queen of heaven right from his father's house. Everybody in his family spoke against him. They sold him. He was persecuted even to the strange land. However, he defeated the queen of heaven in the house of Potiphar as well as in prison. Nevertheless, these days, believers are no more ready to pay the price. They forget that Christianity is not bread and butter; it involves fasting at certain times and praying all night. At times, one needs to pay with one's blood. I am afraid that most of the prosperity in the churches today is from the queen of heaven. She has used many General Overseers, General Superintendents, Bishops and Church Founders to divert their members' worship to herself through false doctrines, worldliness, immorality, love of money, tribalism etc. The queen of heaven is a powerful witch. Only those with God's Spirit can win her if they use divine weapons aright.

If you always stand with God and for God alone, He will give you the hidden treasures of darkness. Ananias and Saphira will no longer keep part of their money if ministers will preach only Christ (Acts 5: 8). When a minister's focus is on money and not on salvation and righteousness through Christ (dupers 419), people will fill the church and refuse to repent. The occult people will become deacons and deaconesses. Pastors will play politics; they will sell and buy in the church; they will use the opportunity of every programme to merchandise in the church. Be careful for nothing; my God shall supply all your needs according to His riches in glory by Christ Jesus in the word of God.

The Lord will give you the treasures of the people of darkness hidden in different warehouses, banks, and government offices in all the nations of the world. It has happened before and can still happen again. Do not limit yourself to the second heaven's "blessings" which come from the queen of heaven. Break into the third heaven (Genesis 47: 15-21). Whatever you are pursuing in this life without Christ, you may get it but it will eventually fail. Is it power? It will equally fail. Money, health, children, education, prosperity etc without Christ will all fail (see Genesis 47: 19). The queen of heaven has purchased many people today for Satan. Many (like Esau) are selling their birthright. Remember Lot's wife (Luke 17: 32). The queen of heaven was the principality that destroyed Lot's wife. She came out from Sodom but her mind, desires, and affections were still there (1 John 2: 15).

Many Christians want to eat their cakes and still have them. It is not possible. You will not succeed in halting between two opinions; you can only serve God or Baal. The people of God in Egypt wanted to serve God and benefit from a satanic government.

But since we left off to burn incense to the queen of heaven, and to pour out drink offerings unto her, we have wanted all things, and have been consumed by the sward and by the famine. Jeremiah 44: 18

The queen of heaven is the goddess of violence. Wherever there is civil unrest, she is in charge. Human life means nothing to her. After all, she did not create them, so she does not lose anything when she destroys them. For those who are faithfully serving her, she uses them and dumps them at will. For those who are uncompromising, she fights them with every available weapon.

When people of God refuse to fight the queen of heaven, they will fight their Jeremiah. They will begin to fight against their church and leaders. Pastors will not work together and there will be division in the church (Jeremiah 44: 15-18). They will argue with their Jeremiahs. They will accuse God. They will give excuses and there will be division. There will be murmuring of the Grecians against the Hebrews. The people will challenge God's constituted authority, and they will leave the word of God to serve stones. There will be famine, poverty, incurable diseases etc.

O God, why hast thou cast us off forever? Why doth thine anger smoke against the sheep of thy pasture? Remember thy congregation, which thou hast purchased of old; the rod of thine inheritance, which thou hast redeemed, this amount Zion, wherein thou hast dwelt. Lift up thy feet unto the perpetual desolation; even all that the enemy hath done wickedly in the sanctuary. Thine enemies roar in the midst of thy congregations; they set up their ensigns for signs. A man was famous according as he had lifted up axes upon the thick trees. But now they break down the carved work thereof at once with axes and hammers. They have cast fire into thy sanctuary, they have defiled by casting down the dwelling place of thy name to the ground. They said in their hearts, let us destroy them together; they have burned up all the synagogues of God in the land. We see not our signs: there is no more any prophet: neither is there among us any that knoweth how long. Psalm 74: 1-9

When people of God refuse to fight the queen of heaven, they enemy will come in with desolation. Her wickedness will be visible. She will take over the pulpit. She will remove signs, wonders and replace them with ensigns. She will promote evil. The pulpit will become witchcraft altar. Burial ceremonies will be greater in number than marriage ceremonies. In other words, there will be more death in the church than marriages. People will be marked for satanic attacks. There will be marks for late marriages. Signs and wonders will be scarce (Psalms 74:9). People will turn churches to ceremonial houses and dens of robbers. There will be divisions. Quarrels and immorality will become an open show without rebuke or remorse (see 1Corinthians 3: 3-4). Instead of preaching Christ, churches will preach against churches. Instead of love, there will be hatred. Instead of demonstrating God's power, Christians will be gossiping and slandering one another and Pentecostal witchcraft will be seen right from the leaders (Nahum 3: 1-4).

When people of God refuse to fight the queen of heaven, the queen of heaven will use people against one another. She will bewitch the church with falsehood, unfaithfulness to God. The result of all these will be multitudes dying without Christ which is the aim and goal of the queen of heaven. Those who are physically alive will be "walking corpses". She normally starts with kings, family heads and women's leaders down to the children's level. Pastors will gossip right in the presence of their children against another pastor or church. That is witchcraft in the church. So many people have left Egypt but Egypt has not left them. Lot's wife left Sodom but Sodom followed her until she died without God. Some great people who have boldly left Sodom are now dying outside Sodom. People are dying right inside the churches today after fighting great battles of faith. Remember Lot's wife; remember Judas Iscariot and make sure you remember Achan, Solomon and others who died without reference to God. Where are you now? Are you still in the faith? Where is your old love? Is your marriage what it is supposed to be? Are you doing your business with the fear of God? Are you among the foolish ones? Is oil still in your lamp? Are you ready to meet the bridegroom? Are you building upon the rock or upon the sand? (Matthew 7: 24-27). Many people are living as if God is not going to ask them for an account of how they lived in this world. The Bible says that every man's work shall be revealed (1 Corinthians 3: 11-15). It is a dangerous thing to forsake God. Willfully committed sin attracts the wrath of God.

Then all the men which knew that their wives had burned incense unto other gods, and all the women that stood by a great multitude, even all the people that dwelt in the land of Egypt, in Pathros answered Jeremiah, saying, as for the word that thou has spoken unto us in the name of the Lord, we will not hearken unto thee. But we will certainly do whatsoever thing goeth forth out of own mouth, to burn incense unto the queen of heaven, and to pour out drink offerings unto her, as we have done, we, and our fathers, our kings, and our princes, in the cities of Judah, and in the streets of Jerusalem, for then had we plenty of victuals and were well, and saw no evil. But since we left off to burn incense to the queen of heaven and to pour out the drink offerings unto her, we have wanted all things and have been consumed by the sword and by the famine. Jeremiah 44: 15-18

For a Christian to stop at a satanic bus stop because of problems amounts to weakness on the part of that Christian. It is a fearful thing to fall into the hands of the living God. The young prophet who entered into rest and ate where he was not supposed to eat was torn to pieces by a lion. He never got back to his destination because he stopped at the wrong bus stop.

For if we sin will fully after that we have received the knowledge of the truth. There remaineth no more sacrifice for sins. But a certain fearful looking for of judgment and fiery indignation, which shall devour the adversaries. He that despised Moses' law died without mercy under two or three witnesses: Off how much sorer punishment, suppose ye, shall he be thought worthy, who hath trodden under foot the Son of God, and hath counted the blood of the covenant, wherewith he was sanctified, an unholy thing, and hath done despite unto the Spirit of grace? Hebrews 10: 26-29

We have to do everything possible to succeed in Christ. There are many roads but only one leads to heaven. The children of Israel and many Christians today retired at ease when the battle of their lives was supposed to begin.

But we will certainly do whatsoever thing goeth forth out of our own mouth, to burn incense unto the queen of heaven, and to pour out drink offerings unto her, as we have done, we, and our fathers, our kings, and our princes, in the cities of Judah, and in the streets of Jerusalem,: for then had we plenty of victuals, and were well, and saw no evil. But since we left off to burn incense to the queen of heaven, and to pour out drink offerings unto her, we have been consumed by the sword and by the famine. Jeremiah 44: 17-18

Any cooperation with the devil can bring temporary prosperity and testimony but by and by, it must be paid for. Nobody has ever received a gift from the queen of heaven without paying for it dearly.

All the incurable sicknesses and the seemingly impossible cases today are from the chambers of the queen of heaven. Such problems and impossibilities have been used by the queen of heaven to torment people and thereby diverted their destines while they were looking for solutions in the wrong places. Most so-called herbalists are the agents of the queen of heaven. It is better to die than to seek a solution from the queen of heaven.

Chapter 6

The Queen of Heaven in the Christian Church

Many modern Christians have forgotten the history of the church. Christ in the Gospel of St. Matthew, hearing the confession of Simon Peter, who openly acknowledged Him{Jesus Christ} as the Son of God, informed him that He would build a church, and the gate of hell would not be able to prevail against. Three things are to be noted: Christ has a church, the church would greatly be impugned by the world, and the uttermost strength and powers of hell, the church would live beyond the attack.

Summarily, the prophecy is categorized in three phases.

1　Christ has set up a church. This needs no declaration.

2　The princes, kings, monarchs, governors, religious leaders and rulers of this world together with their subjects, with all their strength and cunning are determined to attack the church.

3　The church, in spite of all these attacks. The church will stand firmly until the end. She has been empowered to overcome difficulties. This prophecy is being fulfilled today in the course of the church. What we see today in the lives of many believers is disappointing. Martin Luther, a man of great talent, vast in knowledge, great learning and fine culture who challenged the church was excommunicated by the Pope who also ordered the burning of his writings on 15th June 1520 A.D. Luther formally renounced the papacy by burning a copy of the "Papal Bull" in the presence of a big crowd. As he cast the bull into the flames, he said: "As thou has vexed the holy one of God (Christ), may eternal fire vex thee".

April 18, 1521 was the greatest day in Luther's life. The occasion has been described as "one of the sublimest scenes which the earth has ever witnessed, and pregnant with blessings". He was asked the second time to defend his writ-up against the church's doctrines. The streets were filled with spectators while the assembly hall was full of notables. People wanted to see the man described by many as "the devil personified". Windows and rooftops were filled with people because the occasion was indeed historical. A single man had risen in revolt against the church and the state was invoked to quell the revolt. Luther was surprised to see such "pomp and brilliancy" in the hall of assembly. The emperor occupied the principal seat. There were about six electors of Empire, twenty-four dukes, and eight Margraves, all representing world powers and all of them, allies of the church.

And there came one of the seven angels which had the seven vials. And talked with me, saying unto me Come hither; I will shew unto thee the judgment of the great whore that sitteth upon many waters: With whom the kings of the earth have committed fornication. And the inhabitants of the earth have been made drunk with the wine of her fornication. Revelation 17: 1-2

The papacy had always used the government in power to achieve its purpose. The archbishops, bishops and abbots were numbered thirty. Seven ambassadors, papal nuncios, and the deputies of free cities. The proceedings started by asking Luther if he was the author of the writings. Luther acknowledged that he was indeed their author. Luther was asked whether he was willing to retract the doctrines contained in the books, which the church disapproved of, or to defend them in part or in whole. Luther replied thus: "The speech that shook the world, "first in Latin and later in German and it ended thus: "Unless I am in error, for popes and councils have often erred and contradicted themselves. I cannot withdraw for I am subject to the scriptures I have quoted; my conscience is captive to the word of God. It is unsafe and dangerous to do anything against one's conscience. There I stand; I cannot do other wise. So help me God". These bold words caused pandemonium in the place. Dr Eck warned the reformer that the General Council of the church was a much safer guide to truth than one person's conscience.

The Apostles and the activities of the queen of heaven

Women received their dead raised to life: and others were tortured, not accepting deliverance: that they might obtain a better resurrected: And others had trait of cruel mocking and scourging, yea, moreover of bonds and imprisonment: They were stoned, they sawn asunder, were tempted, were slain with the sword: they wandered about in sheepskins and goatskins; being destitute, afflicted, tormented: (of whom the world was not worthy) they wandered in deserts, and in mountains, and in dens and caves of the earth. Hebrews 11; 35-38

The queen of heaven is the goddess that diverts people to demonic destiny. She can offer you anything to take your salvation. To some, people their trial may be cruel mocking; but they should continue to endure and not give up. To some, it may be scourging; but they should also persevere and not give up. To some, it may be bonds; they should continue forbearing and not give up. To some, it may be imprisonment. They should equally continue hoping; and not give up. To some, it may be sickness, but they should keep believing and not give up at all. To some, it may be the temptation of joblessness; they do not have to give up in their search either.

To some, it may be a mark of late marriages; they too do not have to give up. Yet to some, it may be poverty, the should continue to fight and not give up. To some, it may be affliction, they should continue to rejoice and they do not have to give up. To some, it may be hatred anywhere they find themselves. They do not need to give up. To some, it may be famine, they should not give up. To some, it may be tribulation; they should not give up in hoping. To some, it may be distress; they should not give up. To some, it may be persecution; they should not give up. To some, it may be fear of tomorrow, but they should not give up. To some, it may be pressure from families. They should not give up. Whatever may be the reason, Christians should not quit following the Lord Jesus Christ (Romans 8: 31, 35-39).

I cannot imagine you at this time cooperating with the evil queen when the battle is almost ending. The trumpet will soon sound (Rev. 22: 14-17, 20). So do not quit. If you miss heaven because of compromise, whom will you blame? The Lord is coming very soon. The time is almost over. The writer of the book of Revelation almost failed. Towards the end of his life, the Apostle John admired the queen of heaven (Revelation 17: 6). When he saw the power, authority, beauty etc attached to the queen of heaven, he almost missed it (Revelation17: 6) Thanks be to God whose angel intervened (Rev. 17: 7, 15).

The good angel of God rescued John. At the last minute of your stay in this world, the enemy may still come. He will always try to deceive you. This principality destroyed the family of Eli. This principality destroyed Soul. This principality destroyed Solomon ((Kings 11: 1-6). Even in the last chapter of Revelation, the queen of heaven still tried John the beloved. She motivated him to worship an angel (Rev. 22: 8-9).

Who is this John that wrote the book of Revelation whom the queen of heaven almost deceived? Who is this John that the queen of heaven almost influenced in order to add an error into the book of Revelation?

And I saw the woman drunken with the blood of the saints, and with blood of the martyrs of Jesus: and when, I saw her, I wondered with great admiration. And the angel said unto me, wherefore didst thou marvel? I will tell thee the mystery of the woman, and of the best that carrieth her which hath the seven heads and ten horns. Revelation 17: 6-7

And I John saw these things, and heard them. And when I had heard and seen, I fell down to worship before the feet of the angel, which showed me these things. The saith he unto me, See thou do it not: for I am they fellow servant, and of thy brethren the prophets, and of them which keep the sayings of this book: worship God. Revelation 22: 22: 8-9.

.The "beloved disciple" was the brother of James the great. He founded the churches at Smyrna, Pagamos, Sadis, Philadelphia, Laodicea and Thyatira. In addition to the book of Revelation, he was the writer of the gospel of John as well as the first, second and third epistles of John. In Ephesus, he was cast into a cauldron of boiling oil. After the oil had boiled for long time, they still found out that he did not die. His persecutors said: "This one is a witch", and banished him to the Isle of Patmos to be eaten by wild beasts. It was while he was there that he wrote the Book of Revelation.

1 John, who also am your brother, and companion in tribulation, and in the kingdom and patience of Jesus Christ, was in the Isle that is called Patmos, for the word of God, and for the testimony of Jesus Christ. I was in the Spirit on the Lord's day, and heard behind me a great voice, as of a trumpet saying, I am Alpha and Omega, the first and the last: and what thou seest, write in a book, and send it unto the seven churches which are in Asia: unto Ephesus, and unto Smyrna, and unto Pergamos, and unto Thyatira, and unto Sardis, and unto Philadelphia, and unto Laodicea. Revelation 1: 9-11

Nerva, the successor of Domitian, recalled him. He was the only apostle who escaped violent death. He was the only apostle who died a natural death.

Peter

Having been condemned to death, Peter was crucified. Hegessipus said that Nero sought matter against Peter to put him to death. When the people realized this, they begged Peter to flee the city. Peter decided to flee but on reaching the gate, he saw Jesus Christ and Jesus asked him: "Whither dost thou go?" Jesus said: "I am come again to be crucified." Peter realizing the message returned to the city. Jerome said that Peter was crucified at his request by turning his head down and his two legs upside because he alleged he was unworthy of being crucified in the same manner as Jesus. The important thing among believers of those days was understanding God's will. The early Christians faced the battle with all boldness (Hebrews 12: 1-4). Let us continue the battle. The Roman Emperor Nero in 54-68 AD dealt decisively with Christians. He was very wicked and callous. Yet, Christians gallantly defended their faith. Nero punished a class hated for their "abominations" because they believed in Christ and who were regarded as Christians. He killed many of them. In addition, he made them serve as objects of amusement. While some were set on fire, others were crucified.

Paul

Paul the apostle, formerly called Saul, after promoting the gospel of Christ, also suffered persecution under Nero. Abdias declared that Nero sent Esquires Ferega and to inform him of Paul's death, tell me that Paul is dead. They found Paul teaching the people and "desired him to pray for them" that they might believe. Paul told them that soon, they would believe and be baptized at his sepulchre. Then the soldier came and took him to a place of execution. Paul gave his neck to the sword.

Mark

Mark was born of Jewish parents. He wrote the Gospel of Mark with the help of Peter who converted him to Christianity. The people of Alexandria, at the great solemnity of Serapis, their idol, dragged him to pieces. He died under their merciless hands (Heb. 11: 35).

James the Less

James the Less was the brother of Jesus Christ. He was elected the overseer of the church at Jerusalem. He was the author of the epistle ascribed to James in the sacred Canon. At ninety-four, he was beaten and stoned by the Jews; and had his brain dashed out with a fuller's club. Governor Trajan advised against the Christians. His system of punishing Christians was to ask them if they were indeed Christians. If they repeated it three times and refused to curse Christ, they were sentenced to death. However, any Christian who agreed to worship the god of

Rome would be freed. Ignatius, the Bishop at Antioch for about forty years, was the child Jesus took in his arm (Matthew 18: 2). Trajan visited Antioch where he met Ignatius and said to him: "There you are, wicked devil". The queen of heaven uses people and tells them lies. Satan called Jesus devil. Trajan called Ignatius a devil. Ignatius answered: "Not an evil spirit, but I have Jesus Christ in my heart". Trajan said: "Jesus Christ within you? Do you mean he who was crucified by Pontius Pilate? Ignatius replied, "Yes, he was crucified for my sins". Ignatius was then killed by lions. Before he died, he prayed and thanked God (Phil. 1: 23).

Polycarp, an apostle of John who received one of the seven letters sent to the churches in Asia in Rev. 1:1, died after much insult. He was said to be burnt with fire (Rev. 2: 10).

Blandina refused every threat and promises in southern France to worship idols and therefore died by having her throat cut off. In Carthage, North Africa, Vivia Perptue, a young mother, lost her life for Jesus. Another notable martyr was Cyprian of Carthage, who was converted in his late age. He was Bishop in his native city for three years. He was condemned to death by the pro-consul, Galerious.

Galerious: Listen to Galerius, you Thascius Cyprian?

Cyprian: I am.

Galerius:	You have given yourself to be a Bishop to people who do not give service to our Roman god?
Cyprian:	I have.
Galerious:	Your life was long been one of sacrilege. You have constituted your antagonism to the gods of Rome and to be a standard-bearer in heinous offences. You shall be a lesson to those who have been associating with you. Our pleasure is that Thascius Cyprian be executed with the sword.
Cyprian:	Thanks be to God (Rev. 17: 6).

Thousands were killed, beheaded, burnt, and thrown to the beasts, etc; because they refused to give up their faith in Jesus.

(Hebrews 11: 35-38). There is the story of forty Christians who were arrested to be killed in those days. After the death of the thirty-ninth persons, the fortieth denied Christ. One of the soldiers saw what happened to them, how each of the thirty-nine Christians had been accompanied to the glory by an angel. He took the position of the fortieth Christian. He removed his army uniform and wore the Christian martyr's garment, weeping and confessing to the glory of God. If you drop your crown, another person will take it. Crowns are exchangeable (Acts 1: 15-23). These are people who rejected satanic deliverance in order to obtain a better resurrection (Hebrews 11: 35-38).

4

The Queen of Heaven, wife of Satan (Rev. 17)

This chapter says many things about the "great prostitute", "a woman with whom the kings of the earth have committed fornication" and has influenced "inhabitants of the (world) earth with the wine of her fornication" (Rev. 17: 1-2). She is arrayed in purple and scarlet color, and decked with gold, "holding a cup... full of abominations and filthiness of her fornication" (verse 4). The "woman" became drunk (verse 6) and was pictured as sitting upon "people, and multitudes and nation, and tongues" (Rev. 17: 15).

Who is this prostitute? Whom does she represent? Who is this personality of whom her own prostitution is so great? A single woman with whom the kings of the earth have committed fornication with. A woman who was able to influence the inhabitants of the world with the wine of her fornication. A single woman who is arrayed in purple and scarlet color, and decked with gold, holding a golden cup in her hand.

The cup in her hand is full of abominations. The mother of harlots and abominations of the earth, who is she? Being a prostitute, she must be an unfaithful, wanton woman. She is not a faithful, upright royal woman; she is not a true wife. However, who is this woman? She is in evil union with Satan. She is the wife of Satan. A woman, that is in charge of bringing the inhabitants of the world into evil relationship with Satan through evil religion. She is the most faithful personality working with Satan presently.

Israel in her faithfulness to God as a channel of righteousness to the world is seen as the wife of Jehovah (Isaiah 54: 5; Jer. 2: 2-3; Isaiah 62: 5).

Nevertheless, whenever the children of Israel became unfaithful to God, she was seen and regarded as a "whore" or prostitute (Hosea 2: 2-13).

The faithful church today in the New Testament is pictured as "the bride" of Christ (John 3: 28-30; 2Cor. 11: 2; Eph. 5: 22; Rev. 19: 6-9).

Therefore, the great "whore" that sitteth upon many "waters" is the most faithful wife of Satan, a woman who gave birth to all the abominations of the world; she is the false church of all ages. She is the religion without Christ in the whole world. She is the goddess of all false beliefs, the mother of all sinners, mother of liars, as Satan her husband is the father of liars (John 8: 44).

She is the mother of prostitutes (Rev. 17: 5). As I said before, the queen of heaven is the senior or sole administrator in the satanic kingdom. Every other department in the satanic kingdom passes through her office. No department of the satanic kingdom can commit prostitution without her. The prostitute here means evil relationship. Any human being or any other creature that does anything with the satanic kingdom is likened to prostitution. Adam and Eve committed prostitution with the queen of heaven that day they ate the forbidden tree. The queen of heaven being addressed as the mother of prostitutes means that every sin that has been ever committed and that will ever be committed must pass through her office. She is a single woman pregnant with every kind of sin. As no father can give birth to a child alone, so Satan cannot commit sin or influence people into sin without his wife, the queen of heaven, the mother of evil union (harlot).

In verse 5, also the Bible called the queen of heaven the mother of abominations of the earth.

No abomination has ever taken place or will ever take place without the mother of abominations giving birth to it. When a man wants a child, he must get married, and make the wife pregnant and will patiently wait for the wife to be delivered of her child. Therefore, like wise will Satan wait for his wife, the queen of heaven before any abomination will be committed on this earth. The queen of heaven and the satanic government of all ages are therefore in the government of all abominations of the earth. Therefore, they are husband and wife of the evil of the earth.

In the kingdom of God, there is no marriage in heaven; and there are neither males nor females. Angels do not marry. The marriage here is an evil union between Satan and the queen of heaven. The queen of heaven is in charge of breaking good marriages, initiating evil ones and destroying marital lives. She is to Satan what Jezebel was to Ahab; what Delilah was to Samson; what Zipporah was to Moses; what the wives of Solomon were to King Solomon; what Cozbi was to Zimri (Numbers 25: 6-18); what Anthaliah was to her family (Chronicles 22: 10; 11Kings 11: 15-16, 18, 20; 11 Chronicles 23: 12,15); what the daughters of Judah were to their brother (Ezekiel 13: 17-23), Hosea 2: 13, what Saphirah was to Ananias. The queen of heaven was to Satan what Herodia was to Herod (Matthew 14: 1-11).

If there is a woman you can never say no to, watch her" she must have the spirit of the queen of heaven. The spirit of the queen of heaven in women usurps authority from their husbands. It is the spirit that makes a man, a woman; and a woman, a man. Satan is like that to the queen of heaven. Just like Ahab was on the throne but fully subject to his wife's moral power to act and take Naboth's vineyard. He was unwilling to shed blood for the vineyard but his wife Jezebel took his position and acted. The queen of heaven (1 Kings 21: 5-15) does most evil actions ascribed to Satan in the scriptures today, she is the most hidden.

She uses many names to cause war and problems. She was the first woman to apply make-up in the Bible.

And when Jehu was come to Jezreel, Jezebel heard of it; and she painted her face, and tied her head, and looked out at a window (11 Kings 9: 30).

She (the queen of heaven) is the mother of abominations (Revelation 17: 4-5).

Death of the Queen of Heaven, Wife of Satan

Presently, there is a worldwide move towards a union of all denominations and churches. Already the world governments of all the nations of the world are forming one union or the other and the nations are naturally forming two portions called Christians and Arab nations (Muslims). The Muslims are already disagreeing among themselves but with time, they are going to come under one group. In the same way, those who are called Christians are also mixed up.

Among them are different groups also formed by the queen of heaven. They are the occultic groups in the name of churches today. The pantheists, the atheists, the materialist, and other occultic independent groups are scattered all over the world. This disagreement will continue until the rapture takes place, no matter how much the peace makers try.

Immediately the rapture takes place, all these small groups in the Muslim controlled nations will naturally become Muslims or be forced to become Muslims.

The queen of heaven, the wife of Satan will then take sides with the nominal counterfeit church member worldwide and gather then together to pave the way for the anti Christ government. All these nations will fight the Muslim controlled nations all over the world. In the midst of these so-called Christian nations, a personality will arise, the anti-Christ, Satan's man. The queen of heaven is sitting on him (the anti-Christ) now but at that time, he will take his right position and kill the queen of heaven.

So he carried me away in the spirit into the wilderness: and I saw a woman sit upon scarlet colored beast, full of names of blasphemy, having seven heads and ten horns. Rev. 17: 3

This personality will be extremely wise and indued with power by Satan himself. He will be energized and empowered by Satan and so will be one with Satan. He will be set aside and distinct from Satan, yet one with Satan, under his complete control. This anti-Christ will have all the attributes of world rulers before him. This individual will appear in the end to head the gentile power in all nations (Ezekiel 28: 1-10).

This will be one of the few programmes of Satan that will take the queen of heaven by surprise, immediately the queen of heaven sees this willful king (Dan. 11: 36-45)). She will commit fornication with him thinking that she will deceive him like other kings of the world in the past (Rev. 17: 2).

The queen of heaven will enter into union with this man of sin, the anti-Christ. In their agreement, the false apostate religious denominations worldwide will enter into coalition with the worldwide government under the leadership of the anti-Christ who will appear as a savior to the church to fight against the Arab world. Millions will lose their lives. The Arabs will be addressing the anti-Christ/queen of heaven coalition as infidels (Christians) while the coalition group will address them as heathens. However, both parties are on the side of the devil. They will be deceived, each believing that they are fighting a just battle.

In the end, the Arabs will lose the battle. Immediately the Arabs lose the war, the political leader who has deceived the queen of heaven's nominal church world and the government in other nations through a peace programme (Dan. 8: 25) will break his covenant with the nominal church (Dan. 7: 25).

And through his policy also he shall cause craft to prosper in his hand; and he shall magnify himself in his heart, and by peace shall destroy many; he shall also stand up against the Prince of princes; but he shall be broken without hand (Dan. 8: 25).

And it shall speak great words against the most high, and shall wear out the saints of the most High, and think to change times and laws: and they shall be given into his hand until a time and times and the dividing of time (Daniel 7: 25).

The anti-Christ, the ruler, in the beginning of his rise to power, is supported and promoted through the help of the prostitute, the queen of heaven, the corrupt religious system, which probably seeks to dominate the beast as usual (Rev. 17: 2-3). The antichrist will rise in the midst of the corrupt religious nation and will be supported. He will enter into covenant with backslidden religious church nations and Israel. He will be seen as the Messiah to deliver the world from the Islamic terrorist world and will be empowered. He will turn around to give arms to the terrorist to overpower the queen of heaven and the backslidden church nations. As his plans is being concluded, the invisible militant church, believers and all remaining Christians in the world, whose names are written in the book of life will be raptured, cut up and taken out of the world in a moment of time, in the twinkling of an eye. The anti-Christ destroys the queen of heaven so that he may rule unchallenged.

And the ten horns which thou sawest upon make her desolate and naked, and shall eat her flesh, and burn her with fire. For God hath put in their hearts to fulfill his will, and to agree, and give their kingdom unto the beast, until the words of God shall be fulfilled. Rev. 17: 16-17

A peace covenant with Israel will last for seven years, which he will also break after three and half years. There are many things I will not put down here in writing because of some reasons, but try to look close into the world politics, the permanent bodies of the United Nations and the two political parties in America.

And he shall confirm the covenant with many for one week: and in the midst of the week, he shall cause the sacrifice and the oblation to cease, and for the overspreading of abominations, he shall make it desolate, even until the consummation, and that determined shall be poured upon the desolate. Dan. 9: 27

He will at that time introduce idol worship. He sets himself up as god.

And the king shall do according to his will; and he shall exalt himself, and magnify himself above every god, and shall speak marvelous things against the God of gods, and shall prosper till the indignation be accomplished; for that is determined shall be done. Neither shall he regard the God of his fathers, nor the desire of women, nor regard any God, for he shall magnify himself above all. Dan. 11: 36-37

He will then, rule the world without rivals after killing the queen of heaven (Rev. 17: 16-17). He bears the attitude of blasphemer because of his enthronement as god (Ezk. 28: 2, Rev. 13: 5-6). He will be the head of the lawless system. All the pastors now and after with political occult leaders, who have acquired power to perform lying wonders magic rings and triple powers to see for money, wealth and fame will be in charge of the lawless system, working with antichrist. Millions of people will lose their lives during his rule for about seven years. A lot will take place, but he will be stopped by the prince of peace and his judgment will take place at the second coming of Christ (Dan. 7: 22, 27).

Until the Ancient of days came, and judgment was given to the saints of the most High; and the time came that the saints possessed the kingdom (Dan. 7: 22).

And the kingdom and dominion, and the greatness of the kingdom under the whole heaven, shall be given to the people of the saints of the most High, whose kingdom is an everlasting kingdom, and all dominions shall serve and obey him (Dan. 7:27).

By and by, righteousness must be enthroned as Christ takes over and constitutes His messianic authority.

And the seventh angel sounded: and there were great voices in heaven, saying. The kingdoms of this world are become the kingdoms of our Lord, and of his Christ; and he shall reign forever and ever. Rev. 11: 15-17

Today is the day of salvation. Is your name written in the book of life? This is not a church matter. True believers are recognized and registered in the Book of Life by God himself. If you cannot make it now, it will be more difficult then.

If thou hast run with the footmen, and they have wearied thee then how wilt thou do in the swelling of Jordan? Jeremiah 5: 12

Anyone who is not genuinely born again now is taking a very high risk and may pay with his blood when it is too late. We are living in the last of this age. This is the time to prepare in individuals inner holiness to separate from corrupt worldly styles. For those who are already in Christ, we are not to give up. The imminent unannounced, sudden return of Christ is our hope and expectation.

Watch ye therefore, and pray always, that ye may be accounted worthy to escape all these things that shall come to pass, and to stand before the son of man. Luke 21: 36

Characteristics of Evil Women

There are characteristics peculiar to evil women, unmarriageable women who are deceived by the queen of heaven in all generations. Evil women in covenant with the queen of heaven break God's covenant. Below are their manifestations:

1.   They are possessed with strange behavior (Prov. 2:16).

2.   They have plastering lips (Proverbs 2: 16).

3.   They easily forsake good training (Proverbs 2: 17).

4.   They abandon God's covenant too fast (Proverbs 2: 17).

5.   At the hours of deceit, they use sweet tongues (Pro. 5:13).

6.   When scheming to draw people to themselves for destruction, they speak softly.

7.   During attack of their victims, they are easily destructive (Prov. 5:4).

8.   In terms of relationship, they are like a chameleon, moveable and unreliable in character (Prov. 5:6)

9.   Evil women possess mixed character; at times, they are extremely clever, lazy, dullards or very brilliant (intelligent) Proverbs 5:6.

10. In response to God's demand, they are stubornly disobedient or sluggish (Proverbs 9 – 11).

11. They possess proud looking dispositions (Proverbs 6:17).

12. They have sharp lying tongues (Proverbs 6:17).

13. Their hands shed innocent blood (Proverbs 6:17).

14. They indulge in wicked imagination because they posses defiled hearts (Proverbs 6:18).

15. They are very fast, clever and masterful in doing evil (Proverbs, 6:18).

16. They bear false witness and tell unsuspecting lies (Proverbs 6: 19).

17. The sow discord among the brethren (Proverbs 6:19).

18. They entangle people in their words (Proverbs 7: 5).

19. They are very subtle and most of them dress in a nude way (Proverbs 7:10).

20. They are very stuborn and loud (Proverbs 7:11).

21. They have the anointing of walker about, vagabond spirit and inconsistent lifestyle (Proverbs 7: 11-12).

22. They are possessed with fake love, which they distribute from person to person for the purpose of destruction (Proverbs 7: 13-23).

23. Their behavior and actions induce people into all manner of evil (Proverbs 7: 3-23).

24. At times, their speech is soft but in the end, destructive (Proverbs 7: 13-23).

25. They are champions in persuading people to do evil (Proverbs 7: 13-23).

26. Their speech is continually resistible to do evil things (Proverbs 7: 21-23).

27. The have the evil ability to control many men (Proverbs 7: 21-22).

28. They distribute incurable sickness and diseases (Proverbs 7:23).

29. They set traps and put people into them ignorantly (Proverbs 7:26).

30. They wound people's great destinies (Proverbs 7:26).

31. They kill great destined people in all generation (Proverbs 7:26).

32. The drag people down to the chamber's of death and hell (Proverbs 7:27).

33. They are very contentious and ceaseless in abusive language (Proverbs 19:13).

34. They are very brawling in nature (Proverbs 21:9,25:24)

35. Their words trap simple-minded backsliders (Proverbs 22:14).

36. They are evil determined personalities (Proverbs 27:15).

37. Confidence in them is like wind that blows across (Proverbs 27:16.

38. They are very cunning and clever like their mother, the queen of heaven (Proverbs 30:20).

The agents of the queen of heaven break God's covenant with joy. They are very deceitful and wicked. They start relationships with fake humility and full of lies. The end of evil relationships with evil women in covenant with the queen of heaven brings death. The only solution is repentance and perfect separation (Proverbs 5: 3-4).

They destroy their own marriage with their own hands. One of the greatest mistakes of any man is to get married to them. John Wesley was a great minister. He was a real man of God who preached and evangelized effectively. He built up the early Methodist Church. He improvingly built up many lives. He wrote commentaries overall Bible, preached and wrote many life-changing sermons. Yet, he made mistake in choosing a wife. We had better listen to those who have tasted all the things, which we are pursuing today. I am talking about those who have examined the present from the past: from the beginning to the end. One of such people is Solomon, the son of David.

Characteristics of Evil Men

1. Evil men speak froward things (Proverbs 2:12).

2. Evil men leave the paths of uprightness (Proverbs 2:13.

3. They walk in the ways of darkness (Proverbs 2:13).

4. They rejoice to do evil (Proverbs 2:14).

5. They delight in frowardness (Proverbs 2:14).

6. Their ways are crooked (Proverbs 2:15).

7. They are violent and deceitful (Proverbs 16:29).

8. They are very wicked (Proverbs 16:30).

9. The repeat evil matters (Proverbs 17: 9(b).

10. Evil men reject reproof and act foolishly (Proverbs 17:10).

11. They manifest rebellion (Proverbs 17:11).

12. They are slothful and wasteful (Proverbs 18:9).

13. They contend a lot with people (Proverbs 18:19.

14. They tarry long at wine (Proverbs 23:30).

15. Evil men behold strange women (Proverbs 23:33)>

16. Evil men utter perverse things (Proverbs 23:33).

17. Evil men are mostly drunkards and are gluttonous (Proverbs 23:35).

18. Evil men are wise in their own conceit (Proverbs 28:12).

19. Evil men make haste to be rich (Proverbs 28:20).

20. Evil men flatter their neighbors (Proverbs 29:7).

21. They transgress the law of God (Proverbs 29:6).

22. The refuse to consider the poor (Proverbs 29:7).

23. They are scornful (Proverbs 29:8).

24. They keep people's lives restless (Proverbs 29:9).

25. They are blood thirst people (Proverbs 29:10).

26. They utter their entire mind without reserve (Proverbs 29:11).

27. They heap shame on their parents (Proverbs 29:15).

28. They increase the bag of transgression (Proverbs 29:16).

29. They exhibit anger and are very furious (Proverbs 29:22).

30. They manifest a proud spirit openly (Proverbs 29:23).

31. Evil men are unjust and they rejoice in injustices (Proverbs 29:27).

32. They are not contented with one wife or what they have (Eccles. 9:9).

It has been proved from the bible that evil men bear false witness and sow seeds of discord (Proverbs 19: 32-33). King Solomon said: "No matter your wisdom, gifts, position etc., if you commit the sin of adultery, you lack understanding and so destroy your own soul". The queen of heaven can allow you to be recognized, to be rich, to manifest the nine gifts of the Holy Ghost, establish church here and there, and even own the whole world if only you can sell your salvation through one hidden or open sin. Look at some of her characters in men (see Proverbs 12:22).

The men who possess the spirit of the queen of heaven are violent, enticing and domineering (Prov. 16: 29-30).

They are not peaceful (Prov. 16: 29-30). They are unforgiving, unreproveable, rebellious and extremely wicked. Most of them normally fall victim to strange women. They are very unfaithful in keeping promises. They pursue riches at all costs from nation to nation and from place to place (Prov. 26: 12, 20; 28: 20). They show respect to persons in order to get whatever they want.

Consequence of the Covenant with the Queen of Heaven

1) Those who are in covenant with the queen of heaven suffer constant from the spirit of death, gradually or instantly (Prov. 2:18).

2) They reap sudden death (Prov. 2:18. 5:5).

3) Her victims face destruction (Prov. 2:19).

4) Her victims reap confusion on the way of life (Prov. 2:19).

5) They end up in hell fire if they fail to repent (Prov. 2:19).

6) They have the anointing of sluggishness (Prov. 6: 9-10).

7) They normally die in poverty in some areas of their life (Prov. 6:11).

8)   They stick and perish in their iniquity (Prov. 5:22).

9)   The cord of sin holds them captive (Prov. 5:23).

10)   Her victims are deceived to die without instruction (Prov. 5:23).

11)   Her victims go astray in their foolishness (Prov. 5:23).

12)   They are reduced to pieces of bread (Prov. 6:26).

13)   Their great destinies are destroyed (Prov. 6:26).

14)   Their victims carry evil fire in their bosoms (Prov. 6:27-28).

15)   They are never innocent (Prov. 6:29).

16)   Their knowledge and understanding are destroyed with the word of God (Prov. 6:31).

17)   The victims destroy souls recklessly (Prov. 6:31).

Characteristics of Good Women

1.   **Godly** women do everything good to retain their honour (Prov. 11:16).

2.   They love and protect their husbands (Prov. 12:4. 31:23).

3.   They are not abusive especially to their husbands (Prov. 12:25)

4.   They openly commend their husbands and secretly rebuke them when they are at fault (Prov. 27:5. 28:23).

5.   They do not think evil against their husbands (Prov. 31: 10-12).

6.   They are industrious (Prov. 13:13).

7.   They hate laziness (Prov. 31:13).

8.   Good women are not idle people (Prov. 31:14).

9.   Good women give adequate support to their family (Prov. 31:14).

10. They are not discriminative in caring in their house (Prov. 31:15).

11. Good women engage themselves profitably (Prov. 31:16).

12. They are courageous and do not exhibit cowardice (Prov. 31:7).

13. They are always in the spirit (Prov. 31:17).

14. They are heavenly minded and they do everything with eternity in view (Prov. 31:18).

15. Hardship does not intimidate them (Prov. 31:90).

16. They show compassion on people (Prov. 31:20).

17. They are fearless and bold like a lion (Prov. 31:21).

18. They provide for themselves and others (Prov. 31:20, 22).

19. They possess new breakthrough skills (Prov. 31:24).

20. Their works are perfect (Prov. 31:25).

21. Their speech is reasonably spoken in wisdom (Prov. 31:26).

22. Their words are full of kindness (Prov. 31:26).

23. They are not parasites, burden to others (Prov. 31:27).

24. They guide their children in good training (Prov. 31:18).

25. Their works are done excellently (Prov. 31:29).

26. They fear only but God (Prov. 31:30).

27. Their work praises them (Prov. 31:31).

Characteristics of Good Men in All Age

1.   Their joy is full, with only one wife (Prov. 5: 18-19).

2.   They avoid evil relationships with strange women (Prov. 5:20).

3.   Godly men allow God to direct their going (Prov. 5:21).

4.   They retain riches (Prov. 11:16).

5.   They are industrious and not lazy (Prov. 20:13).

6.   They are ready to receive divine counsel (Prov. 20:5).

7.   They are very faithful (Prov. 20:6).

8.   They walk in integrity (Prov. 20:7).

9.   They have blessed children in the end (prov. 20:8).

10.   They wait on the Lord (Prov. 20:22).

11.   They have a plain character (Prov. 27:5).

12.   They abound in divine blessings (Prov. 28:20).

13.   They are very liberal (Prov. 28:27).

14.   They are righteous (Prov. 29:6).

15.   Their life exhibits joy and happiness Prov. 29:6).

16.   They are considerate (Prov. 29:6).

17. They are very peaceful (Prov. 29:8).

18. They are just in their dealings (Prov. 29:10).

19. They are self-controlled in speech (Prov. 29:11)

20. They don't give room to gossiping (Prov. 29:12)

21. Their thrones are established forever (Prov. 29:14)

22. They discipline their children (Prov. 29:15).

23. They wait for God in righteousness (Prov. 29:15).

24. They have a vision (Prov. 29:18).

25. They are not in an evil haste (Prov. 29:20.

26. They train their servants as their own children (Prov. 29:21).

27. They do not exhibit anger (Prov. 29:22).

28. They are humble in spirit (Prov. 29:23).

29. They maintain clear separation from sinners (Prov. 29:24.

30. They fear God and trust him (Prov. 29:25).

31. They depend on God's favour (Prov. 29:26).

32. They are upright (Prov. 29:27.)

33. Their strength is given to God alone (Prov. 31:3).

34. They allow God to choose their wife (Prov. 31:10).

35.   They trust their God given wife (Prov. 31:11).

Chapter 7

CONSEQUENCES OF EVIL PROSPERITY

1. Evil prosperity puts her victims to shame (Prov. 17:13).

2. Her victims end their journey on this earth; they have no record in heaven (Prov. 17:13).

3. The possessors of evil prosperity shall not be honored (Prov. 8:18).

4. Evil riches disappear easily (Prov. 8:18).

5. Prosperity without God is weak (Prov. 8:19).

6. God stays far from their prosperity (Prov. 8:20).

7. Their riches have no divine substance (Prov.8:21).

8. Their treasures shall not give fulfillment (Prov. 8:21).

9. Their ways are possessed by Satan (Prov. 8:22).

10. Evil prosperity shall be wasted (Prov. 8: 23-30).

11. Their treasures profit nothing (Prov. 10:1).

12. God cast their substance away (Prov. 10:3).

13. Their slack hand returns them to poverty (Prov. 10:4).

14. Victims' names shall rot (Prov. 10:7).

15. Their blessings are filled up with sorrow (Prov. 10: 22, 23).

16. The righteous (Prov. 24: 1-2) shall abhor victims.

17. Their house foundation and life are established without considering God (Prov. 24:3).

18. Their establishments are not from God, so they are not established at all.

19. They became possessors of unpleasant riches without divine wisdom (Prov. 24:4).

20. God shall reduce their strength (Prov. 24:5).

21. Wisdom is too high for them; they hasten to prosperity without divine principles (Prov. 24:7).

22. They stick to evil counselors and falsehood (Prov. 24L6).

23. They shall be called mischievous people (Prov. 24:8).

24. They are abominable with evil thought (Prov. 24:9).

25. They shall faint on the day of their life battle (Prov. 24:10.

26. Their joy increases in evil times (Prov. 24:7).

27. The rise of their calamity is sudden (Prov. 24:22).

28. They shall fall for not building with divine plan (Prov. 24:27).

29. Their house shall be made desolate (Prov. 24: 28-34).

30. In times of God's wrath, their riches will disappoint them (Prov. 11:4).

31. Evil riches end victims with death (Prov. 11:19).

32. They shall return to poverty, their evil riches shall not prosper God's programme (Prov. 11:24).

33. They are not liberal to divine work (Prov. 11:25).

34. Victims withdraw their wealth from supporting the people of God and the poor; they are under a curse (Prov. 11:26).

35. They shall receive mischief (Prov. 11:27).

36. They shall fall while trusting in their riches (Prov. 11:28).

37. They will not invest for winning souls to Christ (Prove 11:30).

38. Their wickedness shall never permit them to be established (Prov. 12:3).

39. They shall be overthrown (Prov. 12:7).

40. They shall follow vain persons (Prov. 12:11).

41. They shall be emptied for being rich without God (Prov. 13:7).

42. Their wealth shall diminish (Prov. 13:11).

43. They shall have a hard way (Prov. 13:15).

44. Their harvest shall be poverty and shame (Prov. 13:18).

45. Overthrown and wasted houses shall be their end (Prov. 14:11).

46. Heaviness of heart and sorrow shall end their life (Prov. 14:13).

47. Their evil labour and prosperity will bring them to penury (Prov. 14:23).

48. Their foolishness fools them (Prov. 14:24).

49. Their treasures are full of trouble (Prov. 15:16).

50. Hatred filled their rich dinner with stalled ox (Prov. 15:17).

51. God will destroy their house without mercy (Prov. 15:25).

52. Their houses are troubled by greediness (Prove 15:27).

53. Health will depart from their bones as they end with unpleasant words (Prov. 16:24).

54. Their hoary head is a curse with sorrow (Prov. 16:31).

55. They possess an uncontrollable spirit that speak proudly (Prov. 16:32).

56. Evil wealth exposes victims to satanic attacks (Prov. 18:11).

57. They are haughty and they reap dishonor (Prov 18:12).

58. Evil prosperity exposes their victims to disgrace (Prov 20:11).

59. Evil prosperity fills victims with a mouth full of gravel (Prov. 20:17).

60. Their end does not bring blessings (Prov. 20:21).

61. End of life with want of every good thing (Prov. 21:5).

62. Vanity of treasures tossed to and from into death (Prov. 21:6).

63. They are destroyed by their robbery (Prov. 21:7).

64. Poverty with richness in the end (Prov. 21:8).

65. The righteous shall be ransomed from them (Prov. 21:18)

66. Treasure weakly spent and undesired (Prov. 21:20).

67.	They will realize their foolishness too late (Prov. 21: 30-31).

68.	Names of victims to evil prosperity will be destroyed on earth (Prov. 22: 1-2).

69.	Thorns and snares shall be on the way to victims (Prov. 22:5).

70.	They shall reap vanity and the rod of their anger shall fall (Prov. 22:8).

71.	Whatever they have shall be taken away by God (Prov. 22: 16, 22).

72.	Their soul shall be spoilt by God (Prov. 22: 22-23; 27, 28).

73.	Their waiting end shall be disastrous (Prov. 23:17-18, 20)

74.	Their riches and crown will be too short-lived (Prov. 27: 23-24).

75.	The poor but righteous shall be better than the evil prosperous person (Prov. 28:6) shall.

76.	Their covetousness shall cut their life short (Prov. 28:16).

77.	They shall have enough poverty for not tilling their hard hearts (Prov. 28:19).

78.	They shall not be counted innocent (Prov. 28:20).

79.   Their eyes shall be evil and they shall reap poverty (28:22).

80.   Victims of evil prosperity help wrong people and are cursed (Prov. 28: 27-28).

81.   They shall be destroyed without remedy (Prov. 29:1).

82.   Their security is removed as the wind of judgment blows across their wealth (Ecc. 1:6).

83.   Satisfaction will desert them, as they will not be filled (Ecc. 1:7).

84.   Their labour will be towards evil things only (Ecc 1:8).

85.   Their eyes can never reject seeing or focusing on evil (Ecc. 1:8).

86.   Evil report will feed them always (Ecc. 1:8).

87.   Evil pleasures will be enjoyed in vanity (Ecc. 2:1).

88.   They will fight and possess vanity (Ecc. 2:2).

89.   Great work without eternity in view ends in vanity (Ecc. 2:4, 11).

90.   The victim acquires riches, treasures and all wealth with vanity vexation of spirit (Ecc. 2:4-11).

91.   Great estates, local and international wisdom and knowledge with wonderful experiences of

all kinds without God brings grief and increase of sorrow (Ecc. 2:26).

92. Fruits of evil in their labour shall be their position (Ecc. 2:24).

93. They shall reap travail (Ecc. 2:26).

94. Their wealth is gathered and heaped up for the godly (Ecc. 2:26).

95. They will be engaged in evil work unto destruction (Ecc. 4: 1-3).

96. They shall not have spiritually heavenly-minded children (Ecc. 4: 7-8).

97. Silver shall not satisfy them nor abundance increase (Ecc. 5:10).

98. As they hold their blessing, others will enjoy it (Ecc. 5:11).

99. They will live without God and reap sleepless nights (Ecc. 5:11).

100. Their own riches will hurt them (Ecc. 5:13).

101. Their riches will perish.

102. His riches will not be handed over to their children (Ecc. 5:14).

103. They will die and be buried naked without their prosperity (Ecc. 5:15).

104. They shall labour for the wind (Ecc. 5:16).

105. They shall eat in darkness all their days (Ecc. 5:17).

106. Victims shall end up with much sorrow, wrath and sickness (Ecc. 5:17).

107. God will take away joy from the victims (Ecc. 6:12).

108. Strangers will reap their labor while they suffer (Ecc. 6:2).

109. Evil disease will terminate their life (Ecc. 6:2)

110. Their appetite will not be filled (Ecc. 6: 6-7).

Chapter 8

IMMORALITY AS AN INSTRUMENT OF QUEEN HEAVEN

It is our responsibility to keep ourselves pure in order to keep the world holy and habitable. Right from our family, to church, to the nation and to the whole world, we must not live to defile others (matt. 18:8-10); 1 Cor. 5: 6-7); 8: 8-13; Rom. 14: 13-15, 19-23).(Common sin among youth – Jeremiah 3: 25; Judges 14: 1-3; 11Samuel 13: 1-5; 1Cor. 5: 1).

Breaking the word of God through unholy relationship – boyfriend or girlfriend in immorality is common among youths; but God is not happy about it. It causes destruction down to the root of one's life. The immorality we are talking about includes fornication, adultery, anal sins, homosexual, any sexual relationship outside marriage between two legal man and woman, etc.

An adult who practices immorality is not only a disgrace to God but also to the younger people who are supposed to take examples from such an adult (1Cor. 10:8, 11; 2-5).

A leader who practices immorality is issuing a license to the devil to deal with his followers. Pastors who receive evil gifts from people without knowing how they got these gifts encourage them to do more evil.

The same goes to parents who receive gifts from their children anyhow. Pastors or parents who do not rebuke evil in their churches or homes encourage the people to do (419) fraud or commit immorality. (See Proverbs 9: 13-18; 23: 27-28; 23:3; Lev. 19:29).

Pastors who commit immorality with their members are God's enemies because they are crucifying Jesus Christ on the cross the second time. Any man who forces any woman into sexual immorality is like a man who sins with a woman before her husband or father.

In addition, any so-called Christian, who commits fornication or adultery in the Christian fold, turns God's house and the whole world into a brothel.

Immorality is an increased sin that the queen of heaven has promoted in the last days to overthrow many people's live, corrupt the entire world and send many to an early grave and to hell fire. She is using the leaders of the world to promote the worst abominable part of immorality in order to separate many from God to turn the world into an evil one world organization for the rule of antichrist soon Rev 17:2… Lev 18:22…

False Doctrine and Teaching as an instrument in the hand of Queen of Heaven

If King Solomon could fall from grace, then the teaching of eternal security is a false one. Eternal security is a doctrine of the devil. True security is in Jesus. Solomon backslided and instead of repenting, he was only regretting and teaching.

Backsliding is the act of going back or withdrawing from following the Lord. The major lesson from Solomon's situation is that immorality, adultery, fornication, loss of first love, uncontrollable desire for material wealth, love of the world, loss of vision, over-confidence, over-estimation of one's ability, deviation from the divine standard and self-management, etc draw one away from God.

Any relationship with the queen of heaven makes one lose God's favor and exposes one to satanic oppression.

Causes of Immorality

1.   Love of the world in fashion or dressing (Gen. 38: 13-16; Isaiah 3: 16-26).

2.   Talkativeness or foolish talking (Prov. 7:5, 23; 24:14).

3.   Doubt (James 1:8).

4.   Unnecessary visits (Gen. 34:1-3); II Sam. 13: 16-20).

5.   Sinful imitation (Eph. 4: 17-20; 1Thess. 4: 3-7).

6.   Unholy familiarity (Prov. 5: 3-4; Num. 25: 1-3).

7.   Unbecoming exchange of presents (Exod. 23:8; Ecc. 7:7).

8.   Inability to resist evil desires and accepting it as a nature and Gods will (James 4:7).

For you to be able to keep God's blessings, observe the following:

➢   Maintain a prayerful life (Mark 1: 35, 1 Thess. 5: 17, 1Peter 5: 7-11; Isaiah 40: 28-31)

➢   Watch as you pray (Mark 13: 32-37; Col. 4: 2; Rev. 3: 11, 16:15; 1Cor. 10: 12-13).

➢   Beware of compromise even in little things (Songs 2:15; Prov. 7: 24-27. Luke 16:10; Job 31:1. 32: 21-22).

➢   Lay all things on the altar (Matt. 6: 19-21. Acts 2: 41-47. Phil. 3: 7-11. Acts 4: 31-37.

➢   Abide in Christ (John 15: 1-5. Psalm 108:1. 112:7. 57:7. Job 1: 20-21. 19: 13-27).

Cure for Sin

✓ Repentance (Isaiah 55: 6-7. 1: 16-20. Eph. 5: 3-14. Matt. 5: 29-30).

✓ Dedication (Job 31: 1. Rom. 6: 19. 12: 1-2).

✓ Cleansing in the Blood (Matt. 26: 28. Isaiah 1: 18. 1 John 1:7).

✓ Faith and faithfulness (Mark 9: 23; Judges 11: 35).

The Queen of Heaven in Every Book of the Bible

It is only in the bible, in its sixty-six books, that God reveals this principality, the queen of heaven. No Christian can successfully live a Christian life to the full without a basic knowledge of the queen of heaven and how to deal with her. The queen of heaven is both the reference point and the origin of wickedness in the world as the mother who conceive; give birth to every abomination on earth and Satan as the father. Only the bible has succeeded in exposing her activities and war against humankind. The queen of heaven is anti-God; anti-Christ and anti-man (see Gen. 3: 1-6). Let us now trace the queen of heaven in collaboration with Satan in all the sixty-six books of the bible.

In Genesis, she was the great prostitute, the motivator of sexual immorality and perversion in Sodom and Gomorrah, the goddess of abomination, carnal festivities, worldly dressing and adornment, worldliness, gluttony, unholy marriages as well as selling and buying without God (Gen. 18: 20-22; 19:1-5, 23-26; Luke 17: 26-29,32).

Likewise also as it was in the days of Lot; they ate, drank, bought, sold, planted, built; but the same day that Lot went out of Sodom, it rained fire and brimstone from heaven and destroyed them all.

The queen of heaven is the goddess that binds people in sin. Other evil powers may release their victims but she is always determined to deceive hers until doomsday (Luke 17: 30, 32).

In Exodus, the queen of heaven was the challenger of God:

And Pharaoh said, who is the Lord that I should obey His voice to let Israel go? I know not the Lord; neither will I let Israel go.

What an insult to our God! What an abomination! (Exodus 5:2). She is the brain behind the wasteful of hard labor without adequate reward. She is the goddess that regarded God's word as vain (Exod. 5:9, 13-14, 17-19). She is the mother of all those who fight against God.

The fool hath said in his heart, there is no God. They are corrupt, they have done abominable works, there is none that doeth good. (Psalm 14: 1).

The queen of heaven used Pharaoh until he was destroyed. Watch out so that she will not destroy you.

She is the inspiration of taskmaster. She is the goddess of destruction, death and anti-male seeds.

And he said, when ye do the office of a midwife to the Hebrew women, and see them upon the stools, if it be a son, then ye shall kill him: but if it be a daughter,

then she shall live.

Her agents – Pharaoh and his taskmaster – have all been used and dumped into hell.

And the Lord said unto Moses in Median, go, return into Egypt: for all the men are dead which sought thy life (Exodus 4:19).

She is the great unfriendly friend. God has put enmity between her and the seed of the woman. No matter what she promises you today, she will one day turn against you. She will put her ugly hand in your throat and press your stomach so that you will vomit all that she has given to you as she did to Judas Iscariot.

For he was numbered with us and had obtained part of this ministry. Now this man purchased a field with the reward of iniquity; and falling headlong, he burst asunder in the midst, and all his bowels gushed out (Acts 1:17-18).

In the book of Leviticus, the queen of heaven is the inventor of strange fire, the originator of false doctrines and false worship. She is also the intruder in the Holy of Holies. She is the great apostate, the disobedient priest and the uninvited monster in the house of God. She is the deceiver of ministers, killer of young ministries, defiler of holy altars, destroyer in the house of God and, propagator of false religions.

And Nadab and Abihu the sons of Aaron took either of them his censer and put fire therein, and put incense thereon and offered strange fire before the Lord, which He commanded them not (Lev.10.1).

The queen of heaven has killed and defiled many holy ministers today, yet nobody is courageous enough to challenge the spiritually dead ministers and remove their stinkingness {defilement} from the holy altar. Many dead pastors, dead General Superintendents, dead General Overseers, dead church founders, sons of Aaron, are still occupying pulpits today. All that is left in many pulpits today are dead Nadabs, dead Abihus and their father Aaron: There is no Moses to discipline them. Aaron wanted his children to continue. We are seeing these deadness and defilement of holy altar unchallenged in all churches.

Thanks be to God for some churches today that still have Moses.

And Moses called Misheal and Eleaphan, the son of Uzziel the uncle of Aaron, and said unto them, come near, carry your brethren from before the sanctuary out of the camp (Lev. 10:4).

There may be Mishael and Elzaphan, the sons of Uzziel, the uncle of Aaron in church. However, where is Moses to give the command? In some churches, there are no Mishael, no Elzaphan, only Aaron, and they are still managing. "It is a family church" so all leaders must come from their family, clan or tribe. Whether the people from their tribe are born again or not, it is of no relevance to them. They want to use them as leaders and manage them as captains. No wonder they are always casualties in the army of Christ. Their decadences and deadness bring immorality, sickness and disease to the body of Christ

Then the twelve called the multitudes of the disciples unto them, and said. It is not reason that we should leave the word of God, and serve tables. Wherefore, brethren, look ye out among you seven men of honest report, full of the Holy Ghost and wisdom, whom we may appoint over this business (Acts 6: 2-3).

In Numbers, she (the queen of heaven) was the chief complainant, the ungrateful murmured, and the one who was shedding crocodile tears.

And when the people complained, it displeased the Lord and

The fire of the Lord burnt among them. And consumed them

> that is in the uttermost part of the camp (Numbers 11:1).

She was the goddess of lusts for Egyptian foods and lifestyle (Numbers 11: 4-6, 10). The queen of heaven is the goddess that speaks evil against leadership. The fighter of God's constituted authority. She is the mistress in charge of disunity and breaking of church. She intrudes in the family:

And Miriam and Aaron spake against Moses because of the Ethiopian woman (Num. 12: 1).

And the entire congregation lifted up their voice, and cried and the people wept that night (Num. 14: 1-4. 16:1-35, 41-55. 2:1-5. 21:4-5).

In the book of Deuteronomy, the queen of heaven is a bastard, an illegitimate child, one born out of wedlock. She is a person of incestuous mixture, the son of a prostitute or one born of fornication.

A bastard shall not enter into the congregation of the Lord; even to his tenth generation shall he not enter into the congregation of the Lord (Deut. 23:2).

She is the archenemy of God's people in all generations, the great conspirator:

An ammonite or Moabite shall not enter into the congregation of the Lord; even to their tenth generation shall they not.... Because they met you not with bread and with water in the way. When you came forth out of Egypt; and because they hired against thee Balaam.... to curse thee (Deut. 23: 3-4).

She is the goddess that curses the people of God for no just cause. She is the goddess in charge of all false prophets. She is the ministry that put evil prophets on salary and gives them the reward of divination. *In the book of Joshua,* the queen of heaven is the trespasser, the mistress of all the accursed things, the destroyer of Israel. She is the goddess of besetting sins.

But the children of Israel committed a trespass in the accursed thing.... (Joshua 7:1).

She is the goddess of idolatry, covetousness and stubbornness. The queen of heaven is the goddess that confesses her sins when it has become too late to do so.

And Achan answered Joshua and said: indeed, I have sinned against the Lord of Israel, and thus have I done (Joshua 7:20).

She is the troublemaker of Israel. The goddess that causes people to labor without enjoying the fruit of their labor (Joshua 7: 19-26).

In the book of Judges, she is the Delilah, born and appointed to destroy every Samson. She is the one who seduces men of God:

And the Lords of the Philistines came up unto her, and said unto her, entice him, and see wherein his great strength lieth…Judges16:5

She is the contractor, charged with producing evil information capable of destroying every man of God.

And the lords of the Philistines came up unto her, and said unto her, Entice him, and see wherein his great strength lieth, and by what means we may prevail against him, that we may bind him to afflict him: and we will give thee every one of us eleven hundred pieces of silver (Judges 16: 5-19).

The queen of heaven was the killer of Samson. The only power that could "shave off" the seven locks on every Samson's head (verse 19). She is an evil altar that kills great people.

In the book of Ruth, the queen of heaven is the family destroyer, the great murderer:

Now, it came to pass in the days when the judges ruled, that there was a famine in the land. And a certain man of Bethlehem-Judah went to sojourn in the country of Moab, he and his wife and his two sons. And they took them wives of the women of Moab: the name of the one was Orpah and the name of the other Ruth: and they dwelled there about ten years. And Mahlon and Chilion died also both of them; and the woman was left of her two sons and her husband (Ruth 1: 1-5).

The queen of heaven is anti-male seed. The spirit in charge of killing men and leaving women alive in sorrow. She is the goddess of childlessness, the mistress of barrenness and the hater of children.

In 1 Samuel, the queen of heaven is the evil imitator – the oppose of the government of God – theocracy. From Abraham to Samuel was about 1,400 years of theocratic reign. However, they suddenly demanded a king to be like other nations, an evil imitation.

Then all the elders of Israel gathered themselves together and came to Samuel unto Ramah. And said unto him, Behold, thou art old, and they sons walk not in thy ways: now make us a king to judge us like all the nations.

The queen of heaven is the goddess of impatience. Their judge, Samuel, appointed by God, was still alive, holy and righteous; yet they demanded another leader.

But the thing displeased Samuel, when they said; give a king to judge us. And Samuel prayed unto the Lord. And the Lord said unto Samuel. Hearken unto the voice of the people in all that they say unto thee: for they have not rejected thee, but they have rejected me, that I should not reign over them (1Samuel 8: 6-7).

The queen of heaven is the mistress of monarchy (1 Samuel 8: 11-18). She is in charge of those self-willed and satanically controlled kings (1 Samuel 14:52). In 11 Samuel, she was the power that keeps women barren until death. She is the despiser of the righteousness.

And as the ark of the Lord came into the city of David, Michal, Saul's daughter, looked through a window, and saw King David leaping and dancing. Michal, the daughter of Saul, had no child unto the day of her death (11 Samuel 6: 16, 23).

Those who despise people that serve God in their hearts are incurring the wrath of God. She is the sponsor of assassinations, the killer of Ishboshet in his bedchamber (11 Samuel 4: 5-9). The queen of heaven is the great unfriendly friend and the goddess of disgrace. She is the mother of incest, the goddess of evil love and promoter of violent lust (rape). She delights in breaking the commandments contained in Leviticus 18:11. She is the spirit that hires men to deflower innocent girls. She is the power, which makes people take delight in committing sin. The queen of heaven is the goddess that inspires infatuation and later makes the lover abandons his\ her partner in irredeemable disgrace and in which some cases lead to death. The queen of heaven is the goddess that inspires people daily with evil lust and desire; and after using the victims, she removes the lust and replaces it with perfect hatred in the heart of the so-called lovers. (11 Samuel 13: 15, 28).

Then Amnon hated her exceeding, so that the hatred wherewith he hated her was greater than the love wherewith he had loved her. And Amnon said unto her Arise, be gone (11 Samuel 13: 15).

Now Absalom had commanded his servants, saying, Mark ye now when Amnon's heart is merry with wine, and when I say unto you, Smite Amnon; then kill him, fear not: have not I commanded you? Be courageous, and be valiant (11 Samuel 13:28).

The queen of heaven is immorality personified. She enslaves the will of her victims (Romans 7: 18). She is a dominating tyrant (Romans 7: 14-20). She is an enemy that corrupts moral nature (11 Samuel 13: 1-2, 15). The queen of heaven is the spirit of family destroyers (Leviticus 18: 6-30).

In first Kings, the queen of heaven was the eater of flesh and drinker of blood (1Kings 1: 25-26).

For he is gone down this day, and hath slain oxen and fat cattle and sheep in abundance, and hath called all the king's sons, and the captains of the host, and Abiathar the priest; and behold, they eat and drink before him, and say, God save King Adonijah. But me, even me thy servant, and Zadok the priest, and Benaiah the son of Jehoiada, and thy servant Solomon, hath he not called.

She was so mean and depraved that she desired to have the three-day-old baby divided into two so that neither of the women would have a living child. She is the spirit, which destroys young lives, and children right in infancy – the killer of babies as she sponsors all abortions (11 Kings 6: 26-29; Leviticus 26: 29; Deuteronomy 28: 53-57). She is also the initiator of false worship in Israel, the goddess that made Israel sin. She was the controller of Jeroboam, the son of Nebats who made Israel sin. She was the willful apostate designed to destroy the ten tribes of Israel. The queen of heaven was the deliberate sinner – the power that took counsel but not of Jehovah, the oppose of the Leviticus priesthood. She was the imitator of divine programmers, the spirit of stubbornness and rebellion against the word of God (see 1 Kings 12: 25-33). The queen of heaven is the sponsor of a husband and wife coming together to execute evil plans.

And it came to pass, when Jezebel heard that Naboth was stoned, and was dead, that Jezebel said to Ahab, Arise, take possession of the vineyard of Naboth the Jezreelite, which he refused to give thee for money: for Naboth is not alive, but dead. And it came to pass, when Ahab heard that Naboth was dead, that Ahab rose up to go down to the vineyard of Naboth the Jezreelite, to take possession of it. 1 Kings 21: 15-16

But there was none like unto Ahab, which did sell himself to work wickedness in the sight of the LORD, whom Jezebel his wife stirred up. And he did very abominably in following idols, according to all things as did the Amorites, whom the LORD cast out there before the children of Israel. 1 Kings 21: 25-26

She was the conspirator and killer of Naboth as she sponsored Ahab's covetousness. The queen of heaven is a great sadist. She rejoices at the death of her enemies. She is the promoter of sorrow and depression. She is the enemy of God's prophets. She is the accuser of the righteous. (Kings 21: 20). The queen of heaven is the goddess that makes evil investments for future generations (1Kings 21: 29). She is the power that welcomes babies into the world with evil covenants and curses (11 Kings 10: 6-11).

In the book of second Kings, the queen of heaven is the goddess of leprosy and the spirit of incurable diseases. She is the spirit of ifs" and buts" in the life of a great man. She is the spirit of all round victory "except one". She is the minus in a man's life. She is a shameful spirit. She is the spirit of isolation. She is the stronghold, built to destroy ministries and ministers. She is responsible for the type of "deliverer" or "deliverance minister" who needs deliverance – mighty man in valor, but he was a leper". The queen of heaven was the spirit that dealt with Miriam in Numbers 12:1-16. This was the spirit that cleaved on Gehazi (11 Kings 5: 2-27.

Every incurable disease has its roots in this sickness and the queen of heaven is in charge of incurable diseases. The queen of heaven is the goddess of sin (see Romans 7: 17. Sin is a hereditary evil, which takes its victims downwards. She is spiritual leprosy. Nobody can be a sinner and at the same time God's friend. The need for deliverance from sin is the first message preached in the Christian assembly. Without deliverance from sin, every other testimony of deliverance is temporary. Sin is the genesis of every other human problem. Without a total deliverance from sin, all other steps aimed at deliverance amount to nothing. Man inherits sin before committing it {PS 51:5}

Psalm 51:5 says:

Behold, I was shapen in iniquity: and in sin did my mother conceive me.

In 11 Kings 7: 3, this spirit arrested four men of great destiny. This spirit attacked and killed a king called Uzziah (see 11 Kings 15:5; 11 Chronicles 26: 20).

It is the spirit that makes a man to do thing without seeking God's intention. The queen of heaven led David away from the will of God. She inspired him to engage in an unprofitable census in Israel.

In the book of 1 Chronicles. It was a selfish exercise (1Chron. 21: 1-2, 9-12). The queen of heaven is the goddess, which causes people to displease God (2chron 21:7, 14). Seventy thousand souls were wasted.

The queen of heaven is a bloodthirsty principality and a whoremonger.

In second Chronicles, the queen of heaven is the goddess that brought about evil companionship (11 Chron. 18:1). The queen of heaven is the sponsor of false prophets and the goddess of all white garment churches (11 Chron. 18: 4-5). She is an evil pastor, the general overseer of all white garment churches, which preach prosperity without righteousness. Pastor who prays and blesses fraudulent people are under her whim and caprices.

Anointing and ordaining men with blood money, originated from her activities. It is in such churches you get "Reverends" and "Bishops" who promote discordances in sinful lifestyles, immorality, worldly dressing and unholy competition in the church.

And when thou art spoiled, what will thou do? Though thou clothest thyself with crimson, though thou deckest thee with ornaments of gold, though thou rentest thy face with painting, in vain shalt thou make thyself fair; thy lovers will despise thee, they will seek thy life. Jeremiah 4:30

The queen of heaven hates men who preach brokenness and holiness, without which no man shall see God. She detests ministers who isolate themselves from popular opinion (see II Chron. 18: 6-8, 12-13). While God is looking for men like Michael, able men who fear God; men of truth, men who hate covetousness, the queen of heaven hates them with great passion.

And now, behold, the king walketh before you; and I am old and gray headed; and behold, my sons are with you, and I have walked before you from my childhood unto this day. Behold, her I am; witness against me before the LORD, and before his anointed, whose ox have I taken? Or whose ass have I taken? Or whom have I defrauded? Whom have I oppressed? Or of whose hand have I received any bribe to blind mine eye therewith? And I will restore it you. And they said, thou hast not defrauded us nor oppressed us, neither hast thou taken ought of any man's hand. I Sam. 12: 2-4

This generation is facing a challenge from God to present representatives, men who will not leave the word of God to serve tables, men of honest report, full of the Holy Ghost and wisdom (II Chron. 18: 16-27}. Prosperity is the will of God for every Christian but pursuing this prosperity at all costs, i.e. without Christ, is the spirit of the queen of heaven. A carnal jokes, even during preaching, as is done in many pulpits today is worldliness. The Egyptian ways of dressing like all the "backless", "topless", mini-skirts and blouses that we see in the body of Christ today even by pastor's wife are not for military Christians who want to go to heaven.(see I Cor. 15: 15-52; I Thess. 4: 16-17).

For thy Lord himself shall descend from heaven with a shout, with the voice of the archangel, and with the trump of God; and the dead in Christ shall rise first: Then we which are alive and remain shall be caught up together with them in the clouds, to meet the Lord in the air: and so shall we ever be with the Lord. (I Thess. 4: 16-17).

The queen of heaven is the goddess of carefree life, carelessness, worldliness, worldly pursuit and ambition without reference to God. The queen of heaven is the sodomite spirit in charge of worldly pleasures and enjoyment. She is also the promoter of adultery and fornication, incest, immorality, and even legalized immorality like gay marriage in the church. She is bent on defiling God's house through his children who are not militant in their lives against her scheme. "After all, I am going to marry her". Secret counseling and unchecked lust among leaders, pastors and their members as well as promises and failures in marriages from the pulpits to the pews are some of the works of the queen of heaven.

In the book of Ezra, the queen of heaven was the adversary of the Jews, the persecutor of God's people. She is anti-freedom, the goddess of bondage. She is anti-God and the oppose of God's temple (Ezra 4: 1, 4).

Now when the adversaries of Judah and Benjamin heard that the children of the captivity builded the temple unto the LORD God of Israel (Ezra 4:1), then the people of the land weakened the hands of the people of Judah, and troubled them in building (Ezra 4:4).

The queen of heaven is a petition writer. She is the evil spirit that monitors the acts of men, so that she could capitalize on their mistakes to punish them. She is an evil reporter and the unfriendly friend (see Ezra 4: 2, 16, 24).

Then they came to Zerubbabel, and to the chief of the fathers, and said unto them, let us build with you: for we seek your God, as ye do; and we do sacrifice unto him since the days of Esarhaddon King of Assur, which brought us up hither (Ezra 4:2).

We certify the king that, if this city be builded again, and the walls thereof set up, by this means thou shalt have no portion on this side the river (Ezra 4:16).

Then ceased the work of the house of God, which is at Jerusalem. So it ceased unto the second year of the reign of Darius King of Persia (Ezra 4: 24).

In Nehemiah, she was the internal enemy, the evil agent, the goddess of evil union. She was the communication minister charged with the responsibility of destroying the people of God and their ministry. The queen of heaven was the goddess of executing evil covenant. She is the author of the most fearful letters of intimidation and harassment to frustrate the ministers of the gospel (Nehemiah 6: 17-19).

Moreover in those days the nobles of Judah sent many letters unto Tobiah, and the letters of Tobiah came unto them. For there were many in Judah sworn unto him because he was the son in law of Shechaniah the son of Arah; and his son Johanan had taken the daughter of meshullam the son of Berechiah. Also they reported his good deeds before me, and uttered my words to him. And Tobiah sent letters to put me in fear (Nehemiah (6: 17-19).

She is the goddess that divides God's people and their work.

But it came to pass, that when Sanballat heard that we builded the wall, he was wroth, and took great indignation, and mocked the Jews. And he spake before his brethren and the army of Samaria, and said. What do these feeble Jews? Will they fortify themselves? Will they sacrifice? Will they make an end in a day? Will they revive the stones out of the heaps of the rubbish, which are burned? Now Tobiah the Ammonite was by him, and he said, even that which they build, if a fox go up, he shall even break down their stone. Neh. 4: 1-3

In Esther, the queen of heaven was Haman, the favored one in the kingdom of Ahasuerus. She is in charged with the responsibility of destroying the people of God. She is the spirit of genocide. Any kingdom, power authority or person that wants to wipe out a tribe or nation has the finger of the queen of heaven in their reign. She is a spirit of oppression (Esther 3: 1-2, 9).

After these things did king Ahasuerus promote Haman the son of Hammedatha the Agagite, and advanced him, and set his seat above all the princes that were with him. And all the king's servants, that were in the king's gate. Bowed, and reverenced Haman: for the king had so commanded concerning him. But Mordecai bowed not nor did him reverence (Esther 3:1-2).

If it please the king, let it be written that they may be destroyed: and I will pay ten thousand talents of silver to the hands of those that have the charge of the business to bring it into the king's treasuries (Esther 3:9)

In the book of Job, the queen of heaven is a spirit of frustration that makes a man regret ever being given birth to. She was the tongue that spoke through Job to curse the day he was born, and the night of his conception. The queen off heaven is the goddess of self-destruction (Job 3: 1-11). The assignment of destroying Job was handed over to the second in command to the queen of heaven, leviathan. This is the most wicked principality in the government of the queen of heaven. Satan and the queen of heaven usually delegate authority and supply necessary weapons. They give counsel and sometimes visit the camp of their victims as in the case of Job see Job (1: 6-7).

The work of Satan is to discover a fertile ground, attackable persons, open the door and assign work to the queen of heaven who in turn re-assigns it to the most wicked principality under heaven in the spirit of the leviathan personality. In other words, leviathan reports to the queen of heaven while the queen of heaven is responsible to Satan. Every other thing that took place in the life of Job from Chapter One to Two as far as evil was concerned was done directly by Satan himself. The queen of heaven opened the main entrance door in Chapter Three.

From chapter Four to the day God delivered Job, all the evil actions were, done by the leviathan spirit. Read Job, chapter Forty-One. The only principality that a whole chapter of the bible was dedicated to was leviathan. *In the book of Psalms*, the queen of heaven was the ungodly that does not walk in the counsel of God. She was the power that stands in the way of every sinner from repenting. She leads him or her away from God. She is the goddess that sits in the seat of the scornful. She has no delight in the law of God. She is a covenant breaker, unfaithful partner as well as "the chaff which the wind driveth away" (Psalms 1: 1-4). Psalmist reveals. Look at the end of the queen of heaven and her followers:

Therefore the ungodly shall not stand in the judgment, nor sinners, in the congregation of the righteous. For the Lord knoweth the way of the righteous; but the way of the ungodly shall perish (Psalms 1: 5-6).

There is no doubt that this evil spirit called queen of Heaven has physical beauty. However, this beauty is an instrument in her hand to fatter, to destroy destinies of men. *The book of Proverbs* reveals her greatly in this enterprise. She is a great whore. She is pictured as hot coals of fire. She has burnt many great men and women (Proverbs 6: 24-29). The effect of a wound from the queen of heaven is incurable. She is the destroyer of souls. She is the one who humbles honourable men. She reproaches those who are highly respected. Her mark – visible or invisible – is without permanent cure. In her anger, she empties the catalogue of evil and cruelty The day of her vengeance is destructive. She is a merciless principality. She is not trustworthy. She is an enemy and so should be avoided.

But whoso committeth adultery with a woman lacketh understanding: he that doeth it destroyeth is own soul. A wound and dishonor shall he get; and his reproach shall not be wiped away. For jealousy is the rage of a man: therefore, he will not spare in the day of vengeance. He will not regard any ransom; neither will he rest content, though thou givest many gifts. Proverbs 6: 32-35

Note that the queen of heaven is a spirit. She can appear as a man or woman. She can give woman a man's organ and vice versa. She can make a man love the things that concern women and in the same way make a woman love the things that concern men. She is the mistress of evil transfer (Romans 1: 26-27; Deut. 22: 5).

The woman shall not wear that which pertaineth unto a man, neither shall a man put on a woman's garment: for all that do so are abomination unto the LORD thy God (Deut. 22:5).

She can answer him or her but it is still the same evil personality.

In the book of Ecclesiastics, the queen of heaven is the manipulator of time and the mistress of barrenness. She manipulates a barren woman to be an enemy to her husband when she is supposed to be a friend. She makes them quarrel at the divine hours of conception and settle the quarrel only when the divine days of conception are over. She causes births to take place at the wrong time and gives people wrong parents. She is the goddess of barrenness, abortion, miscarriages and premature birth. She can cause a person to be born at the wrong time, at the wrong place, and in the wrong way. She removes life when it is most needed. She is the goddess of wrong positions in life. Once you are wrongly positioned, you will not be able to fulfill your divine destiny. Are you a professor, lecturing in an institution of higher leaning when you are supposed to be a preacher of the gospel? Are you a preacher when you are supposed to be a banker? God does not bother Himself with blessing or entrusting much in wrongly positioned people.

To every thing, there is a season, and a time to every purpose under the heaven: a time to be born, and a time to die; a time to plant, and a time to pluck up that was is planted. A time to kill and a time to heal; a time to break down, and a time to build up; A time to weep, and a time to laugh; a time to mourn, and a time to dance; A time to cast away stones, and a time to gather stones together; a time to embrace and a time to refrain from embracing; A time to get, and a time to lose; a time to keep, and a time to cast away; A time to rend, and a time to sew; a time to keep silence, and a time to speak; A time to love, and a time to hate; a time of war, and a time of peace. Eccl. 3: 1-8

Every matter in life has an ordained conclusion. How do you conclude and conduct your daily affairs. How do you conduct your daily activities including discussions with your spouse? Is it with the fear of God or with a non-challant attitude to God? How do you carry out your business activities and what is your relationship with the people around you? How do you intend to conclude the last hours you will spend in this world?

Let us hear the conclusion of the whole matter: Fear God, and keep his commandments: for this is the whole duty of man. For God shall bring every work into judgment, with every secret thing, whether it be good, or whether it be evil. Eccl. 12: 13-14

Solomon regretted his actions. Why then do you make him example of your immorality. Having seen it all, Solomon conclude that only the wise uses wealth, beauty, education, knowledge, life etc, to win souls. People call him a wise man but he actually knew who a wise person should be, hence he said: "He that winneth souls is wise." Give Solomon the opportunity to live again and you will see him dedicate it to soul winning, "Vanity of vanity, all is vanity." Anything you are doing without the fullness of God is a useless endeavor and a waste of God's time (Eccl. 12: 1-7).

In the Songs of Solomon, the queen of heaven was "the little foxes that spoil the vines." She is the spirit of it does not matter "She comes subtly to destroy a life. A little drop of her idea in a man's mind can destroy whole destiny. Flee from the queen of heaven and all that represents her. Do not give her any space – no compromise, no negotiations and no agreement whatsoever (Songs 2: 15).

Behold, thou art fair, my love: behold thou art fair; thou hast dove's eyes.

A dose of sexual immorality, a dose of lie will ruin a destiny. It is 100% purity. A little opportunity given to her can wipe out a whole nation or race (Numbers 25: 1-39).

And Israel abode in Shittim, and the people began to commit whoredom with the daughters of Moab. And they called the people unto the sacrifices of their gods; and the people did eat, and bowed down to their gods. And Israel joined himself unto Baal-peor: and the anger of the LORD was kindled against Israel.

And those that die in the plague were twenty and four thousand (Numbers 25: 9).

The queen of heaven is described by *Nehemiah* as an outlandish woman. His contention was that if they could defeat Solomon. She is the spirit of compromise. If she could cause him to sin, pull him away from God, make a caricature of this greatest man of his generation and reduce him to a piece of bread, then she can destroy any life. Thus, she should be seen as an enemy, a viper, a witch that should not live in our midst. She is an altar that should be pulled down and from whom we should flee. It is clear from the account of the scriptures that God loved Solomon. However, a little compromise with the queen of the air irritated God, provoked Him and exposed the man to open shame and satanic invasion. What are you doing with the queen of heaven? You have to come out now by fire, in the name of Jesus.

Did not Solomon King of Israel sin by these things? Yet among many nations was there no king like him, who was beloved of his God, and God made him king over all Israel: nevertheless even him did outlandish women cause to sin. Neh. 13:26

Please answer the question in verse 27:

Shall we then hearken unto you to do all this great evil, to transgress against our God in marrying strange wives?

Brother, how many wives do you have – in your office, house, school, church, place of business etc? Sister, how many strange men do you have? Pastor, how many wives do you have in your congregation? (Matt. 5: 27-28, 31-32).

Before we round off the Songs of Solomon, I want you to see this caution in Mark 9: 43, 45 and 47.

And if thy hand offend thee, cut it of: it is better for thee to enter into life maimed, than having two hands to go into hell, into the fire that never shall be quenched: (Mark 9:43.

And if thy foot offend thee, cut it off: it is better for thee to enter halt into life, than having two feet to be cast into hell, into the fire that never shall be quenched (Mark 9:45).

And if thine eye offend thee, pluck it out: it is better for thee to enter into the kingdom of God with one eye, than having two eyes to be cast into hell fire: (Mark 9:47).

Who is your "hand"? It may be that he/she, the only hand that feeds you. It may be the only hand that supplies your needs. However, if God be God, cut it off. Do not "wound" it, that is not what God is saying. The command is: "Cut it off". Is he/she the only source of your supply? The command still stands: "Cut it off". God is saying that it is better off than in. Who are your feet? What does the bible mean by your leg? It means your long leg. It is that certificate that advertises you; that profession that makes you proud; your vehicle, prosperity, anointing from the queen of heaven, the power you are using to confuse, bewitch or intimidate your congregation, people under you; "Your sugar daddy" etc. Do not wait until tomorrow; do not wait until you finish your education: "cut it off" now. Become lame temporarily. He who demands that you "cut it off" is faithful. He says; it is better. And if He says it is better for you to "cut it off", it is indeed better. So cut it off immediately.

The importance of an eye in human life cannot be over emphasized. However, if the Lord says, "pluck it out", please let us obey him. What is the need of trying to see when one cannot see anything at all? The Lord is in the holy temple; and once He is there, let every other person keep silent. If He says, "cut it off", "pluck it out", there should be no argument. Just obey the Lord. Professor, Preacher, Reverend, Bishops of any level or experience, keep silent (Habakkuk 2: 20).

But the Lord is in his holy temple: let all the earth keep silence before him.

In the book of Isaiah, the queen of heaven is the spoiler of lives, homes, businesses and every good thing. The way occult people destroy lives recklessly portray them as real agents of the queen of heaven. She uses people in the top to spoil others. Native doctors (herbalists), occultic medical doctors, demonized teachers and students in cults in collaboration with the queen of heaven have destroyed many lives. Pastors and members who destroy through gossip, backbiting, slanderers are agents of the queen of heaven. Let it be to you that the power of destruction from the queen of heaven has an expiring date.

Woe to thee that spoilest, and thou was not spoiled; and dealest treacherously, and they dealt not treacherously with thee! When thou shalt cease to spoil, thou shalt be spoiled; and when thou shalt make an end to deal treacherously, they shall deal treacherously with thee. Isaiah 33:1

Whatever you get from the queen of heaven for destructive purposes will also be used to destroy you in the prime of your life. The bible says that you shall reap whatever you sow; and that the same measure you use to others for ritual, at the end of the day, the same thing will happen to you (Isaiah 33:7).

Behold, their valiant ones shall cry without: the ambassadors of peace shall weep bitterly.

In the book of Jeremiah 28: 10-11 and 16-17, the queen of heaven is the deceiver and killer of false prophets. Satan deceives his agents first before he uses them to deceive others. He raises a man, uses him to destroy others and, in the end, destroys the same man.

In Ezekiel 8:14, the queen of heaven is the Tammuz, the goddess that had influence over the women of Israel and other nations.

In the book of Daniel, the queen of heaven is that "image of gold whose height was three score cubits and the breadth six cubits". The queen of heaven is the spirit behind every image being worshipped in many places today. Even some so-called churches are worshipping images today (see Daniel 3: 4-7). The queen of heaven is the goddess of rebellion, the one who makes people depart from the path of righteousness (Hosea 13: 16). She is also the goddess of drunkard mentioned in Joel 1: 5.

Wine is a mocker, strong drink is raging: "and whosoever is deceived thereby is not wise." The queen of heaven used this instrument against the following:

1. Noah   Genesis 9: 20-21

2. Nabal 1 Samuel 25: 36

3. Lot   Genesis 19: 30-38

4. Elah   1Kings 16: 8-10

5. Benhadad   1 Kings 20: 16-21

6. Ephraim   Isaiah 28: 7

7. Belshazzar   Daniel, chapter 5

8. Nineveh   Nahum 1: 10.

In the book of Amos, she is the killer of children in the womb, i.e. the great murderer, destiny quencher and destiny amputator. The queen of heaven is the evil power, which fulfilled the evil prophecy in Hosea 13:16, II Kings 8: 12 and 15: 16.

Samaria shall become desolate; for she hath rebelled against her God: they shall fall by the sword; their infants shall be dashed in pieces, and their women with child shall be ripped up (Hosea 13:16).

And Hazael said, why weepeth my lord? And he answered, Because I know the evil that thou wilt do unto the children of Israel: their strongholds wilt thou set on fire, and their young men wilt thou slay with the sword, and wilt dash their children, and rip up their women with child (II Kings 8: 12).

The Menahem smote Tiphsah, and all that were therein, and the coasts thereof from Tirzah; because they opened not to him, therefore he smote it; and all the women therein that were with child he ripped up II Kings 15:16).

She is charged with the duty of seeing that any curse placed on anybody is fulfilled. She is the executor of curses and evil covenants.

The queen of heaven is the goddess of violence against Jacob and the people of God *In the book of Obadiah* (see Obadiah, verse 10).

For thy violence against thy brother Jacob shame shall cover thee, and thou shalt be cut off forever.

She sponsored and assisted forces against Judah (verse 11).

In the day that thou stoodest on the other side, in the day that the strangers carried away captive his forces, and foreigners entered into his gates, and cast lots upon Jerusalem, even thou wast as one of them.

Her delight has always been to see the downfall of a child of God. She spoke proudly in the day of distress of the people of God (Obadiah, verses 12-14).

In the book of Jonah, the queen of heaven is the goddess of wickedness in all nations (Jonah 1: 2). The queen of heaven is the religious preacher who hates repentance and salvation. She is the one that prefers God's judgment to mercy (Jonah 4: 1-3, 10-11).

But it displeased Jonah exceedingly, and he was very angry. And he prayed unto the LORD and said, I pray thee O LORD, was not my saying, when I was yet in my country? Therefore, I fled before unto Tarshish: for I knew that thou art a gracious God, and merciful slow to anger, and of great kindness, and repentest thee of the evil. Therefore now, O LORD, take I beseech thee, my life from me: for it is better for me to die than to live.

Then said the LORD, thou has had pity on the gourd, for the which thou hast not laboured, neither madest it grow; which came up in a night, and perished in a night: And should not I spare Nineveh, that great city wherein are more than six score thousand persons that cannot discern between their right hand and their left hand; and also much cattle? (Jonah 4: 10-11).

The queen of heaven is the general overseer of all the churches and pastors that curse their member and preach prosperity without salvation. She is the pastor in the congregation of "419", fraudster's members and people with blood money (Amos 2: 6-8).

Thus saith, the LORD; For three transgressions of Israel, and for four, I will not turn away the punishment thereof; because they sold the righteous for silver, and the poor for a pair of shoes; That pant after the dust of the earth on the head of the poor, and turn aside the way of the meek, and a man and his father will go in unto the same maid, to profane my holy name: And they lay themselves down upon clothes laid to pledge by every altar, and they drink the wine of the condemned in the house of their god.

They call evil good; they are men's pleasers (Micah 3: 1-3).

And I said, Hear, I pray you, O heads of Jacob, and ye princes of the house of Israel; is it not for you to know judgment? Who hate the good, and love the evil; who pluck off their skin from off them, and their flesh from off their bones; who also eat the flesh of my people, and flay their skin from off them; and they break their bones, and chop them in pieces, as for the pot, and as flesh within the caldron.

She is the mother of Pentecostal witchcraft. She owns those pastors who preach prosperity while bewitching their members to sow seeds for selfish purposes, enriching themselves while many of their members are poor. One may ask, what is Pentecostal witchcraft, or how does one identifies them? Below are the features that characterize Pentecostal witchcraft.

Chapter 9

CHARACTERISTICS OF PENTECOSTAL WITCHCRAFT PASTORS

1. Their preaching does not touch sins. They do not preach about sin and repentance correctly.

2. They pull the flesh of their members from their bones. They enforces giving either being led by the spirit or not, and they amount demanded or gift coveted is always huge.

3. They eat human flesh and drink their blood through witchcraft

4. The hate good

5. The secretly love evil

6. They commit immorality with their members

7. They lie about God's presence. i.e. They intimate false prophecy, word of knowledge and words of wisdom

8. They 'teach for hire'

9. The take bribes

10. They pervert judgment

11. They divine for money

12. They cry peace, peace but make war on all who do not agree with them.

13. They bite (with their teeth). I.e. they talk evil of others.

14. They easily become angry in the pulpit.

In the book of Micah, the queen of heaven is portrayed as the deviser of iniquity and doer of evil works right from the bed to the office. She is the one who coveted Naboth's vineyard (Micah 2:1-2, 9).

She is seen *in the book of Nahum* as the one contending with God – the archenemy of God (Nahum 1: 9). However, the destruction of the queen of heaven and all her followers will be complete and final. She shall be destroyed as fully dried stubble (Nahum 1: 10-11).But now that she is still alive, she contends with the blessings of God's children.

The queen of heaven is shown as the transgressor, the proud and the coverer of evil *in Habakkuk*. She is also seen as the contractor and Land Lord who built in blood to enrich herself. She "enlarges (her) evil desires – lust of the flesh and lust of the world." The queen of heaven is seen in the book of Habakkuk as death. She can open her mouth and drink the blood of millions of people – yet without satisfaction (Habakkuk 2: 5-6). This is the reason for war in many nations. Whenever, she is thirsty for blood she instigates war. She is the spoiler of many nations (see Nahum 2: 8-12).

In Zephaniah, the queen of heaven is called Baal. Chemarims and host of heaven upon the housetops,

Malcham. She is also the hanging altar. Any charm, idol or object that people look up to in worshipping is the queen of heaven. She is called the fowls of air, the fishes of the sea. She is the creature on these altars, etc (Zeph. 1: 3-5, 10, 18). The queen of heaven is the goddess that makes people rejoice in sin. Careless believers who clap hands and dance disco music in the church after committing immorality are sons and daughters of the queen of heaven (Zeph. 2: 15. 3: 1-4).

In the book of Haggai, the queen of heaven is the goddess of procrastination in the work of God. She is in charge of the slogan "Let me do my business this year before I answer the call of God" (Haggai 1: 2, 4-6). Those who are in this condition should simply leave the dead to bury their dead while they go and preach the gospel (Luke 12: 16-21). The queen of heaven is the goddess that postpones every good thing. She brings fear when one wants to take a good decision. She is the goddess that keeps people where they are not supposed to be. She is the spirit of selfishness. She is the spirit that can allow you to belong to a church but will make you unprofitable to the church and useless to God. The queen of heaven is the spirit that wants help from God and the church without contributing to the progress of the church. She is the spirit of:

- "I want to get married before I become serious."

- "If God gives me a husband, then I will stop dressing like Jezebel" (II Kings 9: 3).

- "I will become a serious-minded Christian when I become a millionaire."

- "If God wants me to go for evangelism, let Him heal me, give me a good job, give me a baby or any child and baptize me with the Holy Ghost."

- "I will work for God when I become the General Overseer of my own church" etc.

- "As soon as I finish my education, establish a good business, get married and train all my children to university level, I will then work for God."

- "When I buy a car, it will be easy for me to go to church."

All these statements come from the queen of heaven. They indicate the presence of the spirit of this queen of heaven in such person's life. (See Haggai 2: 9-11).

As a Christian, endeavor to pay your tithes and give you offerings. It is a sin to "borrow" your tithes from God. It is this queen of heaven that makes people complains in the church: "what are they using our tithes and offerings to do" (Malachi 1: 7-8, 14). These people do not give as they should; yet they are the first to gossip in the church and complain of certain needs in the church. They "gang up" against the leadership of the church (Romans 16:17). This queen of heaven is a terrible spirit attacking churches today.

In the book of Zechariah, the queen of heaven is the spirit of religion without Christ, activities without mercy and fasting and praying without eternity in view. This spirit led the people of God into captivity. In captivity and sorrow, she allowed them to pray and fast every fifth and seventh month with evil feast to her (the queen of heaven)

– Zech. 7: 4-7. The queen of heaven can allow you to sing like an angel, pray like Elijah and Moses, fight and defend the "Virgin Mary" and shout the names of saints many times, dress like a lady on her wedding day, walk sanctimoniously, cast out demons, be recognized by the authorities of your church's general overseer etc but once she knows that you are going to hell because of a particular sin, she can allow you to go ahead (Romans 10:1-3). One false doctrine or besetting sin in your life can take you to hell (see Zechariah 7: 8-12). See also II Kings 18: 33, 41. The queen of heaven is the goddess of divorce and remarriage, the unfaithful partner (Malachi 2: 14, 16. The only type of marriage, which God supports, is monogamy. God is against polygamy. As long as your spouse is alive, no portion of the scriptures allows you to marry another person.

The Queen of Heaven in the New Testament

As we discuss the activities of the queen of heaven in the New Testament, we will go into a little detail in the first four books of the gospel of our Lord Jesus. I told you that the queen of heaven is very secretive. As much as possible, she tries to hide her identity to the extent that people find it difficult to discover her activities in most books of the bible especially in the New Testament. You may not see her name but the character and actions will tell you who exactly is acting. Most attacks and evil done in the New Testament are done by this principality, using any person, kingdom, authority and every available weapon for her operations against the instrument of salvation.

149

In the book of Matthew, the queen of heaven is Herod in wrath, who "sent forth and slew all the children that were in Bethlehem, from two years old and under, according to the time which he had diligently enquired of the wise men." The queen of heaven is the killer of children, the killer of good things. She fulfils evil prophecies (see Matthew 2: 16-18).

The devil appeared in the battlefield in the wilderness to confront Jesus with temptation but he was completely defeated by Jesus with the weapon of the word of God: "It is written." (Matthew 4: 4, 6, 11). I think that the devil left the spiritual wilderness and left the assignment to the queen of heaven who manhandled John the Baptist and cast him into prison and later beheaded him. She is the hater of Jesus who entered into the men of Gergesenes and besought Christ to go out of their coasts (Matthew 8:34). She is the goddess that uses the men of any town to frustrate the gospel of our Lord Jesus Christ. She was the killer of the ruler's daughter who Jesus raised from death. She was the motivator of the Pharisees who said that Jesus was casting out devils by the power of Beelzebub, the prince of devils. She was the real spiritual mother of Herod's daughter who demanded the head of John the Baptist in a charger. She was the unfaithful servant who after receiving forgiveness from his master went and cast his fellow servant into prison for his inability to pay. She was the goddess of the rich young man who went out sorrowfully from Christ and preferred his riches to becoming Christ's disciple.

The queen of heaven is the power that causes people to seek positions like the two sons of Zebedee who demanded to sit at both sides of Jesus without considering the other ten disciples. She is the same power that moved the ten disciples with indignation against the sons of Zebedee with the aim of scattering the disciples. She was the mother of the Pharisees who took counsel to entangle Jesus in a chat by asking whether they should pay tributes to Caesar.

The queen of heaven is the monster that led the Sadducees into a doctrine of "no resurrection." She possessed Judas Iscariot and made him go and covenant with the chief priests to betray Jesus Christ for thirty pieces of silver. The queen of heaven made Peter and the two sons of Zebedee sleep in the battlefield in order to weaken them for the early morning trials of faith in a conflict between the Lord Jesus and all the hosts of hell. She was the unfriendly friend who gave Jesus the last unfriendly kiss on earth. The queen of heaven was the one who weakened Peter for a spiritual battle and prepared him for a physical battle – with a sword in his hand and with which he cut off one of the ears of the servant of the high priest.

The queen of heaven was the multitude, the scribes and the elders who sought false witness to kill Jesus. She was the one that used ordinary creatures to spit on Christ, buffet, smite and mock the creator of humankind. She was the Peter who denied Jesus Christ three times even with an oath. She was the elders of Israel who took Jesus to Pilate the governor. She was also the spirit that used Judas Iscariot and later led him out to where he committed suicide. She was the governor who washed his hands and used the same hand to scourge Jesus thinking that his hands were clean with "holy" water without genuine repentance.

The queen of heaven is the goddess of all those who use "holy" water, anointing oil and Psalm 35 and preach the gospel without genuine repentance. She was the leader of the Roman soldiers who took Jesus to the common hall and stripped off his clothes, and put on Him a scarlet robe on His head, a crown of thorns. She was the soldier that gave Him vinegar and gall to drink instead of the water He demanded. The queen of heaven was the thief at the left-hand side of Jesus who insulted Him, wagged his tongue and insulted Him; saying to Him, "Save thyself, if thou be the son of God, come down from the cross and we shall believe you." She was the chief priest and the Pharisees who called Jesus a deceiver. She was the spirit in them that sealed His grave and set watch over it to prevent the Ancient of Days, the owner of the heavens and the earth from resurrecting. The queen of heaven was the one who took counsel, bribed the soldiers and conspired with them to lie against the resurrection of Jesus Christ.

Hell was let loose when Jesus was born and the focus was to stop Him from going to the cross. All these insults were enough for Christ to turn and command fire to destroy the people he came to save; but He maintained silence, and kept His agreement with His Father in heaven. If Christ had failed, the whole world would have failed. Now, note that some people's destinies are tied together with yours. Therefore, your failure will affect them. What we have to ask ourselves is this: "How did Jesus succeed? What was His response? And how did He handle these situations?"

Read the whole of the New Testament and you will see how he handled seemingly "impossible" situations. This man decided to please God at all costs. In His determination to please God, He took an uncompromising stand in the midst of all His enemies. Jesus was born for the rise and fall of many in Israel. Many people lost their lives – both the innocent and the unrighteous ones – but Jesus persevered even to death on the across. If he had become angry, felt insulted and acted otherwise, the whole world would have perished. However, some died, and many were saved, while still many are yet to be saved.

If we listen to men and circumstances around us like lust of the flesh, lust of the eyes, pride of life, worldly desires, carnal festivities, worldly pleasures, worldly pursuits, unholy ambitions, worldly discussions etc. we will fail God, fail our generation and all the people who are looking up to us and reading us as their epistles. When Christ won the battle on the cross, even His enemies confessed Him to be the Lord and many joined His group on the day of Pentecost. Do not give up; the hosts of heaven are watching you. If you fail, many will perish, heaven will loose and hell will be enlarged. I refuse to populate hell, in the name of Jesus. I will rather depopulate hell, in the name of Jesus. The Queen of Heaven must die. We must rejoice over her. What are you going through now? Others have gone through that and many are still fighting. You are therefore not alone. God still has several thousands who have not bowed down to Baal. If you fail, you will not meet them in Heaven. To overcome, you must be dead to sin, do not set your affection on things of this world. Set your affection on Christ, and get rid of inordinate affection for people or things. The battle will soon be over. In the book of Mark, the queen of heaven is seen as household wickedness. Jesus' countrymen did not recognize Him.

They got offended by Him.

And he went out from thence, and came into his own country; and his disciples follow him. And when the sabbath day was come, he began to teach in the synagogue: and many hearing him was astonished, saying, from whence bath this man these things? And what wisdom is this, which is given unto him, that even such mighty works are wrought by his hands? Is not this the carpenter, the son of Mary, the brother of James and Joses, and the Juda, and Simon? And are not his sisters here with us? And they were offended at him. But Jesus said unto them, a prophet is not without honour, but in his own country, and among his own kin. And in his own house. And he could there, do no mighty work, save that he laid his hands upon a few sick folk, and healed them. And he marveled because of their unbelief. And he went round about the villages, teaching. Mark 6: 1-6

The queen of heaven, as the initiator of all false traditions, she was in the Pharisees and scribes accusing Christ's disciples of breaking their tradition by eating with unwashed hands. She was the tempter of Jesus by seeking a sign from heaven. She was the hater of children who prevented little children from coming to Christ. She is the goddess of stubbornness in children of today. She is the bazaar organizers who are merchandizing in churches today. She is the goddess of selling and buying in the church. She was the moneychanger and dove seller. She was the chief priests and elders in the churches, the old prophets who did not want to recognize the move of the spirit unless it came from them.

She is the hater of true (divine) power that is not approved by the church councils or committees.

And they come again to Jerusalem: and as he was walking in the temple, there come to him the chief priests, and the scribes, and the elders. And say unto him, By what authority doest thou these things? And who gave thee this authority to do these things? And Jesus answered and said unto them, I will also ask of you one question, and answer me, and I will tell you by what authority I do these things. The baptism of John, was it from heaven, or of men? Answer me. And they reasoned with themselves, saying, if we shall say, from heaven: he will say, why then did ye not believe him? But if we shall say, of men: they feared the people: for all men counted John, that he was a prophet indeed. And they answered and said unto Jesus, we cannot tell. And Jesus answering saith unto them. Neither do I tell you by what authority I do these things. Mark 11: 27-33

The queen was the scribes who loved long clothing, recognition in the marketplace, special seats in synagogues and uppermost rooms at feasts. She was the devourer of widows and makers of long formality prayers without genuine salvation. She is the anointed enemy of people who "sponsor" the gospel. She was the spirit in people who displayed indignation against the woman who poured ointment on Jesus to prepare Him for His death. She was the murmured personality in Simon's house against all that contribute to the gospel (see Mark 14: 3-9).

It was the queen that bound Jesus and delivered Him to Pilate and accused Him (Mark 15: 1-36). She was the Pilate who sat on the judgment seat questioning God. Jesus was able to quickly recognize this queen of heaven in many people and that was the secret of His victory. He said: "Father, forgive them for they know not what they do." Jesus decided not to discuss with or answer any question from the queen occupying the judgment seat in the guise of Pilate. Rather, he maintained silence. In addition, whenever He talked, it was not to discuss with the queen or answer her questions. Therefore, it was not Pilate that sat to judge Jesus but the queen of heaven. The weapons of our warfare are not carnal. "Follow peace with all men and holiness without which no man shall see the Lord." (Mark 15: 2, 15).

The queen of heaven was also the passerby who insulted Jesus, and made a caricature of Him by saying to Him:

Ah, thou that destroyeth the temple, and buildeth it in three days, save thyself and come down from the cross … (Mark 15: 29-32).

In the book of Luke, the queen of heaven was the great people, the scribes and Pharisees, the lawyers and professors of those days who rejected the true knowledge and counsel of God.

And all the people that heard him, and the publicans, justified God. Being baptized with the baptism of John. But the Pharisees and lawyers rejected the counsel of God against themselves, being not baptized of him. Luke 7: 29-30

Those people were merrily" educated-foolish" people under the bondage of the queen of heaven. They are ever learning without coming to the knowledge of Christ. She was the disciples who tried to forbid others from casting devils in the name of Jesus. The queen of heaven is the goddess of "as long as you are not a member of our church, you are not going to heaven, even if you are living a Christian life" She is the goddess of one church (Believers' Union, yet without Christ. She is the goddess of unity for evil purpose (Luke 9: 49-50).

The queen of heaven is in charge of all ministers and churches that preach against other true believers in Christ for selfish purposes. She was the disciple that asked Jesus to kill the people he came to save with fire. She is the spirit that loves Jesus but with a hidden agenda. The queen of heaven is the spirit behind the maxim, "God helps those who help themselves." She is the spirit of serving tables at the expense of the word of God. She is also the spirit that makes one so busy that coming to church becomes impossible and takes solace in sponsoring the gospel.

The queen of heaven is the spirit that prefers the kitchen to the pulpit: "I must eat before I go to church even though I will be late".

Now it happened, as they went, that he entered into a certain village: and a certain woman named Martha received him into her house. Moreover, she had a sister called Mary, which also sat at Jesus' feet, and heard his word.

But Martha was cumbered about much serving and came to him, and said, Lord, dost thou not care that my sister hath left me to serve alone? Bid her therefore that she help me. And Jesus answered and said unto her Martha, Martha, thou art careful and troubled about many things: But one thing is needful: and Mary hath chosen that good part, which shall not be taken away from her. Luke 10: 38-42

The queen of heaven was the foolish rich man who was planning without God. She is in charge of those who postpone their salvation until death catches up with them. She is the spirit of sowing without reaping, the spirit of full (or free) born with an empty dining table and prosperity without benefit (Luke 12: 16-21). The queen of heaven is both the terror by night, and the pestilence that walks in darkness. She is the spirit of premature

death; i.e. anti-long life; the spirit that kills immediately prosperity comes. The queen of heaven is the mother of activities without Christ, the spirit that honours every invitation, except divine ones. The queen of heaven is the personality that gives excuse for absenting from holy programmes. She is the chairman of every occasion except the greatest wedding ceremony.

And when one of them that sat at meat with him heard these things, he said unto him, Blessed is he that shall eat bread in the kingdom of God. Then said he unto him, a certain man made a great supper, and bade many:

And sent his servant at suppertime to say to them that were bidden, come; for all things are now ready. And they all, with one consent began to make excuse. The first said unto him, I have bought a piece of ground, and I must needs go and see it: I pray thee have me excused.

And another said, I have bought five yoke of oxen, and I go to prove them: I pray thee have me excused. And another said, I have married a wife, and therefore I cannot come. So that servant came, and shewed his lord these things. Then the master of the house being angry said to his servant. Go out quickly into the streets and lanes of the city. And bring in hither the. And the maimed, and the halt, and the blind. And the servant said, Lord, it is done as thou hast commanded, and yet there is room. And the lord said unto the servant. Go out into the highways and hedges, and compel them to come in, that my house may be filled. For I say unto you, that none of those men which were bidden shall taste of my supper. Luke 14: 15-24

The queen of heaven was the spirit responsible for the demand and wasteful life times of the prodigal son as well as the spirit of "the poor man at the rich man's gate" – the spirit of starvation. The queen of heaven is the spirit that does not want to enjoy itself and angry when others are enjoying at the table of the Lord. It is the spirit that stays outside the gate in time of great feast because of the return of the periodical son. The brother of the prodigal son stays with the father and obeys his father without enjoying the father's great wealth. She is also the spirit that allows a person to receive his or her share of God's blessing and waste it in sin. The queen of heaven is the spirit of "babyhood," a situation where one is always waiting for one's father to give one what one is old enough and even over qualified to take.

Now is elder son was in the field: and as he came and drew nigh to the house, he heard music and dancing. And he called one of the servants and asked what these things meant. And he said unto him, thy brother is come: and thy father hath killed the fatted calf, because he hath received him safe and sound, and he was angry, and would not go in: therefore, came his father out, and entreated him. And he answering said to his father, Lo, these many years do I serve thee, neither transgressed I at any time thy commandment: and yet thou never gavest me a kid, that I might make merry with my friends. But as soon as this thy son was come, which hath devoured thy living with harlots, thou hast killed for him the fatted calf. And he said unto him, Son, thou art ever with me, and all that I have is thine. It was meet that we should make merry and be glad: for this, thy brother was dead, and is alive again: and was lost, and is found. Luke 15: 25-32

She is the spirit that subjects people to suffering not because of their transgressions but because, of their ignorance. The queen of heaven makes people suffer and depend on her instead of on God. She is the spirit that took Jesus to the high mountain, and showed Him all the kingdoms of the world in a moment of time and promised to give the glory thereof to Him if He would worship her (the queen of heaven). This is the spirit that puts people in the kingdom of God, i.e. to be Christians without knowing that all that God has belongs to them (see Luke 15: 31).

And he said unto him, Son, thou art ever with me, and all that I have is thine.

The queen of heaven was the spirit of Nathaniel's "can anything good come out of Nazareth?" "Behold, an Israelite indeed, in whom is no guile." Once you settle the problems of sin in your life, then fight the demonic occupant of your foundation, resist the devil and good things will begin to come out of your Nazareth. Every Nazareth in your life must change because of Christ.

Phillip findeth Nathanael, and saith unto him. We have found him, of whom Moses in the law, and the prophets, did write, Jesus of Nazareth, the son of Joseph. And Nathanael said unto him, Can there any good thing come out of Nazareth? Phillip saith unto him, Come and see. Jesus saw Nathanael coming to him, and saith of him, Behold an Israelite indeed, in whom is no guile! John 1:45-47

The queen of heaven was the unfaithful disciples who followed Christ because of miracles of food. Therefore, once a miracle delays, they go back to the world (John 6:66). She is the invisible hands behind the fornication prowess of the woman who was caught in adultery. Are you a fornicator? Jesus is saying to you, "Go and sin no more" (John 8:1-11). She was the Pharisees that cast stones on Jesus. She was the parents of the blind man from the womb who told a lie and so did not give glory to Jesus in order to retain their position in the church

(John 9: 18:23). She was the Pharisees who reviled the blind man for taking the decision to stand on the side of Jesus even though his parents were afraid. The queen of heaven is the goddess in charge of preventing people from leaving their parents" dead churches. She is ready to kill or destroy in order to put people in fear and bondage of false religions. She is the spirit that knows the truth without saying it. She is the spirit that allows people to go to church as long as they do not identify with Christ. This is the spirit that imprisons people in the synagogue (church) without spiritual life but bound by fear (see John 12: 10-11, 18-19).

She is the spirit that may allow people to go and accept Jesus but remain a secret disciple (John 19: 38). Again, the queen of heaven is the spirit that makes things hard for ministers and sends them back into the world (John 21: 2-3, 14-20).

In the Acts of the Apostles, she was the mocking spirit: "These men are full of new wine". The queen of heaven was the priest's captain of the temple and Sadducees who imprisoned Peter and John (Acts 4: 1-3).

The next day, their rulers, elders and scribes, and Anas the high Priest, and Caiaphas, and John and Alexander and as many as were of the kindred of the high priest, were gathered together at Jerusalem. And, when they had set them in the midst, they asked, by what power or by what name have you done this? (Acts 4: 18, 21-22).

The church leaders were inspired by the queen of heaven to destroy the true believers. She was the Ananias and Sapphirah who lied against the Holy Ghost. She was behind the people who put the apostles into a common prison (Acts 5: 17-20, 27-28, 33). She was the goddess who went into the church, the internal enemy who raised the Grecians to murmur against the Hebrews "because their widows were neglected in the daily ministration. She was the synagogue attendants who disputed with Stephen, told lies against him, stirred up people to give false witness against him, and later stoned him to death.

The queen of heaven was the personality that bewitched the people of Samaria. She was the sorcerer in the person of Simon, who was pretending that he himself was some great one. She was the family spirit of Herod's family who killed James and imprisoned Peter. She is the proud spirit who takes God's glory. She was the real Bar-Jesus, Elymas the sorcerer, seeking to turn away the deputy from faith. She was the power that pulled John Mark out when the going became tough and separated the ministry of Barnabas and Paul with sharp disagreement (Acts 15: 36-39). The queen of heaven is the destiny killer who possessed a damsel with the spirit of divination and made money for her master through soothsaying (see Acts 16: 15, 19-24).

She is the great grand master who donates people to occultic groups to make money and amputate their destinies. She was the spirit that entered into the seven sons of Sceva and at the same time assigned greater demons to the maniac of Ephesus for the purpose of destroying both parties. She was one spirit in the two parties. The queen of heaven is the spirit that makes people call the name of Jesus whom Paul preached without honoring the same Jesus. She is the spirit of nakedness (Acts 19: 13-16). She was the rich merchant at

Ephesus, Demetrius, a silversmith who made silver shrines of Diana and who was the leader of the craftsmen at Ephesus – the greatest worshipper of the queen of heaven (Acts 19: 2328, 34-35, 38).

The queen of heaven was the principality, which made Paul compromise his faith and lower his standard as regards objects of worship (see Acts 22: 17-27). This was the only place where Paul was persuaded and influenced to observe the "traditions of the elders" (Gal. 2: 1-15). From this time, he entered into problems. Ananias, the high priest asked people to smite him (Paul) contrary to the law and Paul's temperament rose and reviled the High Priest, which was also against the law. These were the actions of the queen of heaven in Paul's life. However, thanks be to God for Paul repented immediately.

The queen of heaven was the killing squad of the Jews. She was the more than forty young men who vowed and bound themselves with an oath not to eat or drink until; they had killed Paul. She was the unrepentant enemy seeking to drink the blood of the saints – the band of evil men (Acts 23: 12-13). She was the great orator hired to accuse Paul – the experienced (and organized) conspirator, the Ahitophel spirit in the New Testament, the accuser of brethren (Acts 24: 1-9). The queen of heaven was Tertullus, a representative of sinners in Israel. The queen of heaven was the goddess that postponed salvation in the life of Felix the spirit that demanded bribes before justice would be done. She was also the willing spirit to do favour to the sinning Jews. The queen of heaven was the spirit in Festus who said that Paul was mad. "And when it was determined that

Paul should sail into Italy he was delivered unto one named Julius, a centurion of Augustus' band. Immediately the entered into the ship the winds became contrary."

The queen of heaven is the goddess of contrary winds. Between Jerusalem and Rome, hell was let loose and all the hosts of hell were loosed. Every power under the leadership of the queen of heaven was ready to terminate Paul's life. Sea monsters were mobilized against Paul and the people with him. The powers of marine in Jerusalem wanted Paul dead. The powers of hell in the seat of the Roman government having heard about Paul did not want Paul alive in Rome. The said forces gathered and agreed that they would meet and fight it out at the centre of the sea. However, the higher power whose ambassador Paul was, was equally ready to defend Paul and get him to Rome alive to fulfill his destiny. The lower and the higher powers met at the high sea (Acts 27: 4, 7, 10, 13-16, 20, 23-25, 40-44).

Verse 14: says: "But not long after there arose against it a tempestuous wind called Euroclydon." Euroclydon was an ancient term for an eastern storm, what modern people call levanter, a typhoon, whirlwind or hurricane blowing in all directions. This was an attack from a crossroads altar. This ship was caught in the hurricane and driven to wherever the wind would take it, an island on the south-the west coast of Crete, now called Gaza.

But not long after there arose against it a tempestuous wind, called Euroclydon. And when the ship was caught, and could not bear up into the wind, we let her drive. And running under a certain island, which is called Clauda we had much work to come by the boat. Which when they had taken up, they used helps, undergirding the ship; and fearing lest thy should fall into the quicksand's, strack sails, and do were driven. And we being exceedingly tossed with a tempest, the next day they lightened the ship; and the third day we cast out with our own hands the tackling of the ship. And when neither sun nor stars in many days appeared, and no small tempest lay on us, all hope that we should be saved was then taken away. Acts 27: 14-2

Marine powers are very stuborn and wicked. Few things happened when Paul escaped the power inside the water:

✓ The queen of heaven quickly entered into an evil counselor who advised the centurion to kill Paul (Acts 27: 42-43).

✓ The evil queen then entered into a viper and got fastened on Paul's hand (Acts 28:3-6). Eventually, Paul got to Rome safely, and the Lord granted him favour before the authorities of Rome.

In the book of Romans, the queen of heaven was the religious Jews who trusted in keeping the Law of Moses as a basis for salvation. She is the goddess of religion without Christ (Romans 2: 21-24).

For the promise that he should be the heir of the world was not to Abraham or to his seed through the law, but through the righteousness of faith.

See Romans 5: 1-2. The queen of heaven is a false teacher and an advocate of sin after salvation."

What shall we say then? Shall we continue in sin that grace may abound? God forbid. How shall we, that are dead to sin, live any longer therein? (Romans 6:6-7).

She was the immoral queen who committed fornication in the book of *1 Corinthians 15: 1, says:*

It is reported commonly that there is fornication as is not so much named among the gentiles, that one should have his father's wife.

In II Corinthians, the queen of heaven was the mother of evil communication. She was the goddess of unequal yoke with unbelievers as well as fellowship of darkness and light (see II Cor. 6: 14-16).

She was the troubler, the perverter of the gospel of Christ *in the book of Galatians.* She was also the Pentecostal witch assigned to bewitch the church of Jesus at Galatians.

In the book of Ephesus, the queen of heaven was the goddess, which limited the Christians and blocked them from praying through Christ but rather through saints (Ephesians 2: 19-20).

In the book of Philippians,

She was the enemy of the cross.

Brethren, be followers together of me, and mark them which walk so as ye have us for an ensample. For many walk, of whom I have told you often and now tell you even weeping, that they are the enemies of the cross of Christ, whose end is destruction, whose God is their belly, and whose glory is in their shame, who mind earthly things (Phil. 3: 17-19).

In Colossians, she was the philosophy that spoilt men after the tradition of men, and after the rudiments of the world, and not after Christ (Colossians 2:8).

In Thessalonians, the queen of heaven was the queen that kept the people of God in ignorance about the rapture of the saints (I Thess. 4: 13-17).

She was also the mother of "them that obey not the gospel of our Lord Jesus Christ" – *in the book of II Thessalonians.*

The queen of heaven was the "position seeker" in the church of Jesus Christ *in the book of I Timothy* (see I Timothy 1: 6-7). She was also the power that turned people away from Paul *in the book of second Timothy* (II Timothy 1: 15). She was Hymenaeus and Piletus who were teaching people against the doctrine of resurrection (II Timothy 1: 12-18). She was Demas who forsook Paul (see II Timothy 4: 1*).

In the book of Titus, the queen of heaven was the unruly, vain talker and deceiver (Titus 1: 10-11).

In the book of Philemon, she was the unrepentant Onesimus, a robber who refused to turn to his creator (Phil. 8:10).

The queen of heaven was the bed defilers, whoremongers and adulterers *in the book of Hebrews* (see Hebrews 13: 4-5).

In James, she was the sinner in times past and sinner in the present – she was the unrepentant monster (I Peter 4: 3) *in the book of I Peter;* while in Second Peter, she was "the false prophet among the people" and "false teacher among you" (see II Peter 4: 1), She is the spirit of "I know Christ" (I John 2: 4, 9, 11, 15-17) but lack His power.

In the book of second John, she was the transgressor that did not abide in the doctrine of Christ (II John, verse 9). She was "Diotrephes, who loves to have pre-eminence among them" *in the book of third John* (see III John 9).

In Jude, the queen of heaven was ordained for condemnation (see Jude verse 4)

For there are certain men crept in unawares, who were before of old ordained to this condemnation, ungodly men, turning the grate of our God into lasciviousness, and denying the only Lord God, and our Lord Jesus Christ.

She was the spirit behind those angles who kept not their first estate but left their own habitation (Jude 6, 8, 16).

And the angels, which kept not their first estate, but left their own habitation, he hath reserved in everlasting chains under darkness unto the judgment of the great day (Jude verse 6).

Likewise also, these filthy dreamers defile the flesh despise dominion, and speak evil of dignities (Jude verse 8).

These are murmurers, complainers, walking after their own lusts; and their mouth speaketh great swelling

169

words, having men's persons in admiration because of advantage (Jude verse 16).

In the book of Revelation, the queen of heaven was the church planted at Ephesus who left their first love (Revelation 2: 4-6). She was the goddess at the Pergamos church with the doctrine of Nicolaitanes and Balaam (Revelation 2: 14-15). At Thyatira, she was the "Jezebel" allowed to prophesy, teach and to seduce God's people to commit fornication and eat things sacrificed to idols (Ref. 2: 20-21). The queen of heaven was the spiritually dead church at Sardis (Ref. 3: 1). She was the liar in the church at Philadelphia, the brethren who said that they were Jews but committed evil (see Rev. 3:9). The queen of heaven was the church of Laodiceans that was lukewarm (neither cold nor hot) and boasting to be rich and had need of nothing (Ref. 3: 15-16). The queen of heaven is the moon goddess that controls confused dreams, water dreams, the seas and every power under the waters. While she controls the waters in heaven, she also controls the water under the heavens through major marine power called the leviathan spirit and the queen of the coast.

Chapter 10

LEVIATHAN AND THE QUEEN OF THE COAST

Who is Leviathan?

Leviathan was the main power that Satan used in attacking Job. He is the demon prince, which controls all marine spirits in warfare. Like the queen of heaven, he is much hidden. Leviathan was mentioned only at the end of the book of Job. Leviathan brings about the actual occurrence of accidents, sicknesses, diseases, and other calamities. Then, he would cause men to believe that God brings these things to pass.

Leviathan makes men blame God erroneously for what he {Leviathan} does. It is very difficult to separate the work of leviathan from that of Satan, the queen of heaven or the queen of the coast. All of them use human beings as agents, as well as serpents and other creatures like crocodiles, cats and dogs. They use the elements and any other creature they can lay hands on (Rev. 12:9). Whatever happens, their works are the same. The only truth is that Satan can raise people and give them power to destroy men and destroy the power they received from the queen of heaven, leviathan, queen of the coast etc – just to confuse people. Their purpose is the same. The queen of heaven can raise armed robbers, powerful native doctors, politicians, and evil men of different levels with the promise that they are above every type of destruction. They may reign and enjoy their powers but at the peak of their popularity, Satan or the queen of heaven may withdraw that power or raise up another group or person to disgrace that personality or authority in a moment. When HIV\AID came, she dominated every other sickness and ruled over every disease. She was on top, reigned and made caricature of every medical approach. We ever sleeps with her victims was affected and tormented unto death. She reigned and ruled until Ebola came and separated her victim, chased them out from their own houses, quarantined them out of sight and dealt even with the medical personals that dared touch her victim.

People who seek power, protection, wealth, prosperity and other quick solutions from Satan, the queen of heaven may get them, but as quickly as the solution may seem to come so also the solution can disappear and the problem multiply. The queen of heaven may assure one that such person is the greatest without requesting any permission from the power{queen of heaven}Satan may decide to raise somebody else to destroy such man. Anything you receive from Satan, the queen of heaven, leviathan, the queen of the coast or any satanic authority can be withdrawn at any anytime, or another power could be raised against you to destroy that power or you without any notice.

Today, even HIV\AID victims are afraid of Ebola victims, even the medical science in the world put together. Ebola is worst than racist and she does not respect any racist law because presently, no court of law, police and the combined military force of any nation can judge her or arrest her but God can.

Will he make many supplications unto thee? Will he speak soft words unto thee? Will he make a covenant with thee? Wilt thou take him for a servant forever? Wilt thou play with him as with a bird? Or wilt thou bind him or thy maidens? Job 41: 3-5

The wicked manifestations of the spirit of Leviathan cannot be quantified. Below are some of the features that characterized his operation in a life or group of people.

Unfaithful and Deceptive. Leviathan is never faithful. He can enter into a covenant with you and breach it the next moment, but if you breach the same covenant, you will pay dearly for it, it may require your life or your offspring. He does not make supplication or suggestion. His words are a command to his victim. If he says, "kill", you have no excuse. He is a *senior partner* in any covenant, and usually, he goes into such a covenant with hidden agenda. He does not accept the position of a servant, son, equal partnership, friendship etc. Leviathan is extremely wicked and destructive.

Shall the companions make a banquet of him? Shall they part him among the merchants? Job 41: 6

He is not friendly to anybody. When God puts enmity anywhere, nobody can bring friend ship out of it.

And I will put enmity between thee and the woman, and between thy seed and her seed: it shall bruise thy head, and thou shalt bruise his heel. Genesis 3: 15

Once wicked leviathan takes a decision, no companion can appease him. Every sacrifice will fail. You cannot persuade him to change his mind. Nobody without Christ can resist him.

Behold, the hope of him is in vain; shall not one be cast down even at the sight of him? None is so fierce that dare stir him up: who then is able to stand before me? Job 41: 9-10

Any power or personality scheming to deceive or overpower leviathan without Christ is simply deceiving himself (Job 41: 27 – 30).

He esteemeth iron like straw, and brass as rotten wood

Pride

Leviathan is very proud. He is the king of all that are proud today (see Job 41: 34).

He beholdeth all high things: he is a king over all the children of pride.

Destructive

Leviathan has raised many powerful men and women and has also destroyed them. He has raised many nations and destroyed them too. Leviathan has made many promises to people and failed. He raised Hitler, Alexander the Great, Herod, Nebuchadnezzar, Cain, Abiram, Balaam, Zimri and Cozbi. He raised Achan, Jezebel, Sennecherib, Haman, Judas Iscariot, the scribes in the days of Jesus, the thief on the cross, Ananias and Saphira, the seven sons of Sceva, Alexander the coppersmith who did Paul much evil, Diotrephes etc.

"A certain rich man which was clothed in purple and fine line, and fared sumptuously every day." No sickness and no lack for even one day; yet he died and went to hell with eternal regret. You may be enjoying yourself without Christ, but one day, you will die. You may have everything you need now, yet one day, you are going to die. You may be a minister of God without any problem and without Christ. I want to tell you that the greatest problem in life is life outside Jesus Christ.

Marine spirit in Many Nations (Isaiah 14: 29; 30: 6)

The queen of heaven uses leviathan to establish international powers, nations, and continents in evil.

Who is Leviathan in the spirit world?

Leviathan is the head of all the python spirits. She is the controller of all python spirits in the whole universe. All satanic kingdoms use python spirits or serpents. Leviathan lives in the high sea where she controls other serpents like flying serpents in the air, serpents in the jungle, serpents in the lands and serpents in the seas. The python spirit is another powerful marine agent but she is still under the family of leviathan. The study of the marine kingdom is very vast. Leviathan supplies serpents to satanic kingdoms, the queen of heaven, the queen of the coast and other satanic kingdoms when the need arises.

Flying serpents or pythons established the nations of Egypt, Assyria, Elam, Meshack, Tubal, Babylon etc in the past and from the same leviathan government, another python or serpent was sent to overthrow and destroy them.

A possessed person can therefore have a serpent from Satan, the queen of heaven, leviathan spirit, the queen of the coast etc. when they are talking through the possessed individual. They can talk according to what they know about the kingdom where they are coming from. Let nobody be confused when they talk; all that we need to do is to cast them out using the name of Jesus (Mark 16: 17).

1.   *Egypt:* This was the power that raised Egypt under the leadership of a great king Pharaoh. She supplied all their needs, raised Egypt, and the king above other nations. However, she later destroyed the people and they are now in hell fire (see Ezekiel 32: 1-2, 21, 19).

And it came to pass in the twelfth year, in the twelfth month, in the first day of the month, that the word of the LORD came unto me, saying, Son of man, take up a lamentation for Pharaoh King of Egypt, and say unto him. Thou art like a young lion of the nations, and thou art as a whale in the seas: and thou camest forth with thy rivers, and troubledst the waters with thy feet, and fouledst their river (Ezekiel 32: 1-2).

Whom doest thou pass in beauty? Go down and be thou laid with the uncircumcised (32: 19).

The strong among the mighty shall speak to him out of the midst of hell with them that help him:

they are gone down; they lie uncircumcised, slain by the sword (Ezekiel 32: 21).

2. *Assyria* (Ezekiel 32: 22-23)

Asshur is there and all her company, his graves are about him; all of them slain, fallen by the sword; whose graves are set in the sides of the pit, and her company is round about her grave: all of them slain, fallen by the sword, which caused terror in the land of the living.

Assyria, which once ruled the whole world and caused terror in the land of the living, is now in hell fire. There is a great question in verse 19.

3. *Elam* (Ezekiel 32: 24-25, 19)

There are Elam and all her multitude round about her grave, all of them slain, fallen by the sword, which are gone down uncircumcised into the neither parts of the earth, which caused their terror in the land of the living; yet have they borne their shame with them that go down to the pit (Ezekiel 32: 24-25).

"Elam which caused terror in the land of the living yet have they borne their shame with them that go down to the pit". They are all in hell fire now, with hot iron beds, in the midst of the slain-defeated ones. Their terror was tough in the land of the living, yet they were defeated.

4. *Meshech and Tubal* (Ezekiel 32, 26-28, 19)

There is Meshech, Tubal, and all her multitude: her graves are round about him: all of them uncircumcised, slain by the sword, though they caused their terror in the land of the living. And the shall not lie with the mighty that are fallen of the uncircumcised, which are gone down to hell with their weapons of war; and there their iniquities shall be upon their bones, though they were the terror or the mighty in the land of the living. Yea, thou shalt be broken in the midst of the uncircumcised, and shalt lie with them that are slain with the sword.

They are all in hell fire now, though they constituted terror in the land of the living.

5.   *Edomites* – Ezekiel 29: 19.

6.   *Zidonian* (Ezekiel 32: 3, 19)

There be the princes of the north, all of them, and all the Zidonians, which are gone down with the slain; with their terror they are ashamed of their might; and they lie uncircumcised with them that be slain by the sword, and bear their shame with them that go down to the pit. They are all in hell fire now, ashamed of their past.

7.   *Satan and all sinful nations* – see Psalm 9: 17, Rev. 20: 7-10. 18: 21-23.

The wicked shall be turned into hell, and all the nations that forget God (Psalm 9: 17. In addition, when the thousand years are expired, Satan shall be loosed out of his prison. Moreover, shall go out of deceive the nations, which are in the four quarters of the earth. Gog and Magog to gather them together to battle: the number of whom is as the sand of the sea. And they went up on the breadth of the earth, and compassed the camp of the saints about, and the beloved city; and fire came down from God out of heaven, and devoured them. And the devil that deceived them was cast into the lake of fire and brimstone, where the beast and the false prophet are, and shall be tormented day and night forever and ever (Revelation 20: 7-10).

And a mighty angel took up a stone like a great millstone, and cast it into the sea, saying, thus with violence shall that great city Babylon be thrown down, and shall be found no more at all. And the voice of harpers, and musicians, and of pipers, and trumpeters, shall beheard no more at all in thee: and no craftsman, of whatsoever craft he be, shall be found any more in thee; and the sound of a millstone shall be heard no more at all in thee: And the light of a candle shall shine nor more at all in thee: and the voice of the bridegroom and of the bride shall be heard no more at all in thee: for thy merchants were the great men of the earth: for by thy sorceries were all nations deceived.

Are you proud of your profession? Professions will soon have no meaning any longer (Ezekiel 32: 19). Leviathan is in charge of all occultic church, evil altars like astral altars and marine altars. Leviathan has links with all secret cults/societies, renowned native doctors or herbalists, occultic hospitals, occultic maternity homes, both small and big organizations that operate without due reference to Christ. Many institutions have been captured. He is in charge of national and international crime. He influences nations to pass laws that are contrary to those of God (see Job 41: 33-34).

Upon earth there is not his like, who is made without fear. He beholdeth all high things: he is a king over all the children of pride.

He is the power behind international wars. He has no boundary in international waters. He uses the serpents, creeping serpents, water serpents and desert serpents. He can operate on both the land and sea. Human life does not mean anything to him. Leviathan hates men especially those that profess Christ. He spreads incurable diseases. Leviathan is the god of death and hell. He reports to the queen of heaven and to Satan – both of whom work hand in hand to fight God and His people.

Dealing with Leviathan

In that day the LORD with his sore and great and strong sword shall punish leviathan the piercing serpent, even leviathan that crooked serpent; and he shall slay the dragon that is in the sea. **Isaiah 27: 1**

The followings should be noted in dealing with Leviathan.

1)   The day you give your life to Christ. God will begin to deal with your leviathan.

2) The day you have knowledge about your leviathan, God will begin to deal with your leviathan in the sea of your life.

3) The day you begin to pray, directing your prayer against leviathan, your leviathan will become uncomfortable.

4) The day you begin to fast and pray, you leviathan will lack water. Science tells us that, about seventy percent of our body is made up of water. Fasting keeps the leviathan spirit, queen of heaven and all marine kingdoms uneasy.

5) The day you believe and practice deliverance, you leviathan will be disorganized.

6) The day you overcome sin and begin to live a holy life, a life of brokenness, your leviathan will lose hold over your life.

7) The day you get tired of your situation and invite God into the battlefield of your life, He will break the head of your leviathan (see Palm 74: 13-14).

8) The day you begin to dry evil waters in your life, God will starve your leviathan (Psalm 104: 26-27).

9) The day you wake up and put on the garment of warfare, your dragon will die (Isaiah 51: 9).

10) The day you pray and get immersed in the Holy Ghost, the Lord will put a hook in the jaws of your dragon and he will die.

Speak, and say. Thus saith the Lord GOD; Behold, I am against thee, Pharaoh king of Egypt, the great dragon that lieth in the midst of his rivers, which hath said, My river is mine own, and I have made it for myself. But I will put hooks in that jaws, and I will cause the fish of thy rivers to stick unto thy scales, and I will bring thee up out of the midst of thy rivers, and all the fish of thy rivers shall stick unto thy scales. Ezekiel 29: 3-5

If you are ready to pray in Gethsemane with Christ all night, by morning, your leopard will die. The Lion of Judah will swallow up your fake lion; the serpent of Pharaoh will be swallowed up by the serpent of Moses.

Chapter 11

QUEEN OF THE COAST

This is an attack by a jealous and wicked female or male-like spirit desiring to marry or be married to human beings. This is the genesis of all resulting in evil marriages with evil spirits – spirit husbands and spirit wives. The queen of the coast is a bit less limited than the queen of heaven and the leviathan spirit in the hierarchy of satanic forces.

Modus operandi of Queen of the Coast. The queen of the coast controls territories with territorial spirit in charge of a particular place. She controls local leaders, family and community shrines. She promotes boundary disputes in order to supply blood to marine blood banks. She controls evil clubs and gives people traditions and customs. She is in charge of community or group compulsory worship and sacrifices to bring people into collective captivity.

Then Nebuchadnezzar in his rage and fury commanded to bring Shadrach, Meshach, and Abednego; these men, O king, have not regarded thee; they serve not thy gods, nor worship the golden image, which thou hast set up. Daniel 3: 13

See also Colossians 2: 8, 16, 23.

Beware lest any man spoil you through philosophy and vain deceit, after the tradition of men, after the rudiments of the world, and not after Christ.

Let no man therefore judge you in meat, or in drink, or in respect of a holyday, or of the new moon, or of the Sabbath days: (Colossians 2: 16).

Which things have indeed a shew of wisdom in will worship, and humility, and neglecting of the body, not in any honour to the satisfying of the flesh (Colossians 2: 23).

The queen of the coast is in charge of ancestral curses and covenants. She controls local streams, altars, etc and gives people laws on whether to kill fish there or worship the creatures or even the water. She controls many evil hair salons, haircut salons, restaurants, market unions, etc. She is the marine personality that captures people for Satan from the grassroots, from the womb and infant stages. She has more agents than every other marine power. While leviathan coordinates people en masse, the queen of the coast starts with an individual right from the womb. She forms a group and hands it over to the leviathan spirit for higher evil operations. She is in charge of evil age-grades. She inspires innocent people to go into groups and invisibly sits with them to influence their decisions. That is the danger of belonging to any gathering without full reference to Christ. Any unbelieving group, no matter how morally good the original initiators may be without Christ, such group will eventually come up with a law or belief that will consciously link them with the queen of the coast. The queen of the coast is a trusted marine power in the kingdom of Satan. She is the early morning evil in the lives of innocent souls (see Psalm 144: 7).

Evidence of Captivity to the Queen of Heaven

1. The victim will be wedded to a water spirit personality.

2. There will be closed doors to true or physical marriage.

3. It also causes terrible marital instability.

4. There will be marriage "break-ups."

5. There will be barrenness.

6. Victims will be bearing polluted children, i.e. strange children or children with abnormal behaviour.

7. Uncompromising victims are always frustrated in life.

8. The queen of heaven usually keeps victims in touch with her agents only.

9. Victims are sexually manipulated, defiled and polluted for God's use.

10. Victims of the queen of heaven are also maritially caged, bound and engaged.

11. All efforts by victims to succeed in life will fail to yield the desired results.

12. Things happening to victims will have no natural explanations.

13. Children of victims will be uncontrollable, stuborn and disobedient.

14.   There will be persistent problems.

15.   Victims are usually marked for evil, hated and are always separated from true sincere helpers.

A Christian with such problems:

1.   Cannot enjoy his or her Christian life.

2.   Cannot pursue a good venture to a successful end.

3.   Will experience difficulties in his or her spiritual life of fasting and prayers will be difficult; serving God and living a holy life will be impossible.

4.   Will display anger and irritation at the slightest provocation or even when nobody offends him or her.

5.   Is obviously proud, pompous and manifests unbelief towards the true doctrines of God.

6.   Will be full of lust – uncontrollable desire for sexual immorality.

7.   Will discover that water dreams will be common in his or her life.

8.   Will be having sex in dreams.

9.   Usually eats in dreams.

10.   Will be catching fish in dreams

11. Will be picking snails in dreams.

12. Will be counting cowries in dreams.

13. Will be having mysterious marriage or engagement breakages.

14. Will find it difficult to get a true-life partner.

15. Is also a victim of curse of non-achievement.

16. Will be exposed to attacks from other marine agents.

17. Will be experiencing a mysterious folding of businesses.

18. Will experience a mysterious loss of good jobs.

19. Will experience a mysterious loss of money.

20. Will become a victim of unexplainable barrenness.

21. Will have miscarriages.

22. May have painful menstruation.

23. May not have menstruation at all.

24. Will have mysterious loss of pregnancies.

25. May have prolonged pregnancy.

26. May have prolonged labour.

27. Will have consistent child delivery via caesarean section.

28.   Will have incurable sickness.

29.   Is often exposed to disasters.

30.   Will lose the desire for marriage but not for the sake of the gospel.

Chapter 12

ENCOUNTER WITH THE QUEEN OF HEAVEN

And after these things, I saw another angels come down from Heaven, having great power, and the earth was lightened with his glory. And he cried mightily with a strong voice, saying, Babylon the great is fallen, is fallen and is become the habitation of devils, and the hold of every foul spirit, and a cage of every unclean and hateful bird. For all nations have drunk of the wine of the wrath of her fornication, and the kings of the earth have committed fornication with her and the merchants of the earth are waxed rich through the abundance of her delicacies. And I heard another voice from heaven, saying. Come out of her, my people, that ye be not partakers of her sins, and that ye receive not of her plagues. Revelation 18: 1-4

For deliverance from the queen of heaven, know the following facts and be conscious of them always.

a.   Recognize her kingdom as a fallen kingdom.

b.   See her as the god of a foul spirit.

c.   The queen of heaven is a cage of every unclean and hateful bird.

d.   You need to come out of her bondage immediately.

e.   Do not fear the queen of heaven.

f. If you die as a victim or as an agent, you will go to hell.

So, fight it out now that you are still alive.

g. Jesus has given us power over unclean spirits including the queen of heaven. Therefore take the following steps:

> Repent thoroughly and truly (I Sam. 7: 3-4)

And Samuel spake unto all the house of Israel, saying, if ye do return unto the LORD with all your hearts, then put away the strange gods and Ashtaroth from among you, and prepare your hearts unto LORD, and serve him only; and he will deliver you out of the hand of the Phillistines. Then the children of Israel did put away Baalim and Ashtaroth, and serve the LORD only.

> Renounce all manner of connection and dedication to the queen of heaven.

> Raise a lamentation against her.

> Cry for your deliverance.

> Pray aggressively and persistently until you are delivered.

> Fast and pray earnestly.

> Go for deliverance.

- ➤ Match righteousness with positive confession.

- ➤ Have faith in God and in your prayers.

- ➤ Preach the bible and give testimonies.

Remember that if you are afraid of the queen of heaven, you cannot defeat her. If you are a friend to the queen of heaven, you cannot also fight her. And if you are not ready to fight her, you will not get your freedom. Job fought her without knowledge and faith. Job did not have enough weapons, but you have the name and blood of Jesus in addition to many other weapons. You can use the weapons of confusion, whirlwind, unbearable heat, blindness, and concentrated acid, the anger of the Lord, great furnace, air quake, seaquake and fire of God. You can use great earthquake, horrible tempest, thunder and fire, sulphur and brimstone, madness, red-hot charcoal, continuous plagues, failures, mistakes and self-destruction. You can use the weapons of fear of day and night, destruction, hail and fire mingled with the blood of the lamb, shock, water of affliction, internal confusion, civil wars, etc. In fact, you can use everything created by God as a weapon against the queen of heaven.

After all, the Bible says in Psalm 24: 1-2:

The earth is the Lord's and the fullness thereof; the world and they that dwell therein. For he hath founded it upon the seas, and established it upon the floods.

Chapter 13

War against the Queen of Heaven

Christianity started by warfare, has since continued in warfare, and will end by warfare. A cousin of mine repented in Kano State in Nigeria because as soon as I became born again, I started praying for all my relatives. This cousin of mine was zealous for God. Therefore, he started preaching everywhere as commanded by the Lord Jesus Christ. Everybody around him knew he was born again – both friends and enemies. As usual, he went out to preach one morning (about 4 am). Some Muslim youths ambushed him and beat him up mercilessly.

They continued to beat him until they were convinced that he was dead. They attacked him with sticks and stones. He lay in a pool of his blood before they left him – thinking he had died. Nevertheless, after they had left, he managed to get to his house. For many days, nobody from his church visited him. Since he had left all his worldly friends and the brethren he looked up to never showed up, he suffered starvatation. He was unable to stand up, take his bath or do any other thing.

For many days, he was without food and water. After many days, he decided to end it up with Christ. As a new convert, he was very disappointed with Christ and Christians in his church. He doubted all he knew about Christ and all the love of God preached in his church. He then decided to burn his bible and die. He picked his bible and was reaching out for a matchbox when a voice told him: "Before you burn this Bible, why don't you open and read just a verse?" After struggling with the Holy Ghost, he decided to read a verse. As he opened the bible, his eyes were "magnetized" to a particular verse. According to him, he tried to avoid looking at that verse but he was unable to do that.

He then decided to read that verse in II Timothy 3: 12:

"Yea, and all that will live godly in Christ Jesus shall suffer persecution."

He then began to ponder on the verse: "Is it true? Is God talking to me?" The verse became so real that he decided to put it to the test. He then said: "O God, if this is true and you are the one talking to me, before I finish reading this verse again, I want you to give me a plate of hot jollof rice." In addition, immediately after that statement, he heard a knock on his door. A woman from his church came with a big plate of hot Jollof rice. This cousin of mine is now a minister of the gospel – happily married with children. Christianity started with warfare and must continue like that until we see our Lord and saviour Jesus Christ.

I was asked to pastor a particular church in my local government. The particular evening I arrived in the town, after preaching, I was ushered into a very small rectangular room. That night, I could not sleep until morning. I complained to the people about the attack by mosquitoes and they told me they were not aware of such a thing in that town. For about one week, I was under severing attack by mosquitoes, which by my estimation were millions in number. I would hear the noise of these mosquitoes, but without seeing or killing even one of them. I almost died within one week of my stay because of invisible satanic attack. I was very sick. I had a temperature. Under this condition, I did not need to be told before I decided to run away. I got tired of that town within one week. The bed I was sleeping on, the walls trees and everything in that town rejected me. To worse the matter, the god of that town, an animal (animal altar), visited me from time to time, to make my life more uncomfortable. The people of that town worship green snake (even up to now). Moreover, it is a taboo to kill that type of snake there. It is believed that if one kills it, one would die or killed physically by the community. The dead snake would be buried with a coffin, clothes and other things used in burying human beings.

There would also be; a period of mourning for the dead snake as if it were a human being. The presence of the snake on my room always made life uncomfortable for me. When I complained, the woman in whose house I lived, would come and beg the snake to leave with praises, as he would be calling the snake their grandmother. The snake would then go out only to come back after a short while. The town was highly occultic. Few pastors who had ever preached there were coming from outside to preach and go. The few Pentecostal pastors from other churches who were living there had no testimony.

Our membership was about seven adults, made up of four old women, two girls and a young man who was healed of madness. The church I was with then had never had a resident pastor before my arrival in that town. I later discovered that our church came to that town through my property owner – who was a priestess of a marine altar. Where marine spirits were being consulted and worshipped. Her first son repented and took the woman to a retreat programme when she was about to die. She was prayed for there and from the retreat ground, the church decided to start a Bible Study in her sitting room. All the pastors who knew the community refused to go and work there. We resorted to sending people from the district headquarters who just went there, taught and left the community immediately. I later discovered also that in almost every quarter of the town, there was a marine spirit church with a priest/priestess.

Members of these marine churches were bold enough to go out for evangelism. They sang all the songs we usually sing in the church, but the difference was that where we put the name of "Jesus", they replaced it with Eze-nwanyi – i.e. Queen of the sea. They meet mostly on Fridays. Therefore, if somebody tells you, "I am going for Friday," you will simply understand that he or she is a member of a marine church. After about seven days, I ran away from that town – even without telling my District Pastor. I ran to Enugu where I stayed for another one week to recover and prepare for my second missionary journey.

As a young man full of zeal, I refused to be defeated. I repented in Lagos, Nigerian, as a young man with zeal to preach the gospel to my people. I left Lagos against the wishes of my people. When I declared that I was ready to work for God at all costs, my district pastor asked me to go to that town as a pastor because of the zeal in me. I had boasted of my God and I promised

God that I would never disappoint Him. I declared to everybody including my district pastor that I could go anywhere. I then decided to go back to the town after about one week. By the time I went back, I was ready for two things – life or death. In addition, because there was nobody to give me accommodation elsewhere, I still went back to the evil altar apartment. The greatest problem I had in that town was seeing a snake around and inside my room, yet I was not allowed to kill it.

However, I decided to endure it for the sake of the gospel. After about six months, one Sabbath man who lived outside but was a native of the town gave me a room in his house. There in the house, I met another Sabbath man. The life of that man "challenged" me. However, I did not believe in his mode of worship, his prayer life challenged me. This man was a man of prayer and his room was next to mine. This man would go inside his room on a Sunday morning and would only come out the next Sunday morning. In addition, while there, he would be groaning and making incantations.

Although I did not like his doctrine, I decided to do something. Other people whose prayer life challenged me were my district pastor, my prayer partner and fellow pastor – a higher schoolteacher then. By the grace of God, the three of us along with many others were used to challenge the powers of darkness in that local government. The result was that by the time we parted in 1997, the Lord had established about thirty-two churches in that district. In that year too, my district pastor was posted out, our district was elevated to a region while I was also made district pastor- before the Lord asked me to leave the district.

My prayer partner also left at that time. These two brothers were mightily used to challenge my prayer life. The Sabbath man who lived in the same house with me was also a big challenge to me. I asked myself, "How can a heathen, an uncircumcised person, do more than a true Christian?" I then decided to pray more than that man did. With the name of God being blasphemed in the town, I decided to challenge the powers of darkness. Therefore, I started fasting. By the time I had fasted for about one month, nobody asked the members of the church to join me before they did.

On the fortieth day of the fasting, the spiritual climate became too hot for the prince of that town. Prayers were going on day and night, and morning cries were organized to be done in the front doors of those marine churches, Sometimes, those evil priests would come out and beat our brethren, curse them and abuse their pastor. These fasting, prayer and morning cries continued in the town until the elders and the native doctors in the town began to do sacrifices in order to appease the god, who they claimed, said that "church people" in the town had driven her out of the community.

In those days, I would not go out to preach unless on invitation because young men and elders were waiting for me to talk so that they would deal with me. I usually went from my house to the church and back; and everywhere I was, prayers would be going on. By the fiftieth day, a very big python was seen in a big river, which formed a natural boundary between the community in which I was pastoring and a neighboring one; and it was facing the latter. That river altar is where they worship a particular goddess called Nmamu. People from various places use to come to see the big snake (Python) in the river. At night the presence of the snake would supply bright light to the place (see the book of Job 41: 19-21, 31-32).

Out of his mouth go burning lamps, and sparks of fire leap out. Out of his nostrils goeth smoke, as out of a seething pot or caldron. His breath kindleth coals, and a flame goeth out of his mouth (Job 41: 19-21).

He maketh the deep to boil like a pot: he maketh the sea like a pot of ointment. He maketh the path to shine after him; one will think the deep to be hoary (Job 41: 31-32).

Sometimes, the snake would disappear and turn into a tall fine young girl with very long hair, so long that it would be touching the ground, and the 'girl' would be facing the river. At other times, it (the python) would change to an old wretched woman. It continued like that until the thing was almost approaching the other town. Nevertheless, another man of God from there, my prayer partner, declared prayer, fasting, and the monster disappeared. By the sixty-first day of our fasting, people began to come to the church uninvited.

One of my relations who was very zealous without Christ became discouraged this time in the school where he was studying to be ordained a "Brother" in the Roman Catholic Church. He came out and said he wanted to enter the monastery to die for our family. After talking to him, he surrendered to the Lord Jesus

Christ. In addition, today, he is an evangelist, prophet and a missionary traveling from one African country to another for the sake of the gospel. At the time of writing this book, he lives in Liberia. He is the founder and the General Overseer of Jesus Prayer Army International, Monrovia. When I was pastoring in that town, an occultic society normally gathered to worship and hold their meetings in that town from almost all the places in the eastern part of Nigeria. They usually met in a very big hall. In fact, the biggest hall in that town at that time. I wrote letter and gave it to their leader asking them to surrender the key of that house for Christian service since they were not serving the true God. That man was one of the most occultic men of our time. He married two women of the same parents (sisters). One day, while we were on evangelism, some of our brethren went to preach to him.

He was upstairs talking to them on the ground when I passed. However, when I finished preaching and was going back, I still saw our brethren magnetized at the same spot. I sensed danger and went inside the compound. I did not talk to our brethren who were standing speechless listening to the occultic man. I looked up at the man and said, "Sir, how can I offer you these tracts?" In addition, he pointed to the staircase. As I was climbing, it was as if I was in a big ocean as the whole place was turning my head.

Nevertheless, I managed to climb and gave him the tracts. By the time we started talking about Christ, he maintained the view that being born again meant baptism and nothing more. At the end of our discussion, he thanked me and advised me to train people well before sending them out to preach. I came down, released my people and we left together. When I wrote a letter to him asking for the hall, my hands nearly got paralyzed. I did not know anything about deliverance then: neither did I know much about evil altars. It is now that I understand that they might have deposited my letter on their evil altar in order to summon my hand. Thanks be to God that my hand was not paralyzed. However, I suffered severe pain in my right hand for a long time; I was fasting regularly at times for three days and three nights; and at other times within that period, for seven days and seven nights without even a drop of water.

One weapon the marine spirit used against me was *witchcraft* attack, poverty and isolation from good things. She took all helpers away from me. I became isolated and ostracized to suffer. By 1990, all my pairs of trousers were torn, likewise all my shirts. There was no money with which to meet my basic needs. The few opportunities I had demanded my backsliding. The old widows and few students that were in the church needed help just as I did. In those days, it was a miracle for me to eat once or twice a day. The leader of the women – a widow who normally gave me food – was somebody who came out from one of the marine churches there. She preached to the priestess who warned her to come back to the marine church or face the wrath of the gods. She was attacked to no avail. In fact, most of our members then were people who came out from that group when they saw that their leader could not bring this sister back despite her boasting and strong determination to do so. A particular boy that came out nearly died from a marine spirit attack. The marine powers afflicted him with chickenpox in addition to other ailments.

At that time, I had not known the principles of deliverance as I do now by the grace of God. Therefore, it took us many battles to keep a member in the faith when he or she left the marine church. One day after our church planting, I came back late and I went to the women's leader but there was no food in her house. I then went to my house and slept off. After about an hour, I heard a knock at my door and I opened the door. It was the last born of the woman in question (a girl) who brought food for me. I could not remember whether I prayed but I finished the food. All through that night, I suffered terribly from internal heat, which was all over my body. By the grace of God, I survived that Saturday night.

Early in the morning, I went straight to the women's leader and narrated my ordeal. She was very sorry and I told her that I was suspicious of her daughter. The daughter was called for interrogation but she denied ever poisoning the food. The mother then brought a cutlass and threatened that if she did not say the truth, she would be killed. She then admitted that as she came out that night with the plate of food, a girl from the marine church came to her and said that she would follow her. According to her, the girl wanted to put something in the food but she resisted it. They struggled until they came to my house. She said that by the time they arrived, I was in deep sleep. Therefore, she decided to climb the dwarf wall into the compound. She then dropped the food by the wall and began to climb. By the time she was climbing, the girl had poisoned the food. Moreover, as a small girl, she was afraid of taking the food back or telling me the problem. Therefore, she came alone to my room and I ate the poisoned food. It was only God who saved me that day. The girl also told us how she had been going to secret meetings with those marine agents.

Before the incident, at our retreat ground, the mother had a dream in which a woman was disputing with her insisting on taking one of her pairs of slippers. As she was struggling with the woman, she woke up. We knew neither the interpretation nor the implication of the dream. This girl then told us that in their meeting, they agreed to give her an incurable wound in one of her legs. In addition, since then one of her legs had an injury. I myself had spent some money for medication to make sure that the injury was cured, but all was in vain. At a stage, everybody got tired of the injury. She also told us that the marine church members agreed to give her that injury because her mother had left them and was then fighting against them. They therefore wanted the woman to be wasting her money through that incurable disease. She revealed to us other children in our church who were their members. I did not understand deliverance the way I now know it now; but with the little knowledge I had then, I prayed and that was the end of the injury – no medication any longer.

At that time, things were too bad for me no food, no clothes, no good accommodation etc. A sister in our church gave her six-spring bed to me. It was a bed she used during her secondary school days. She also offered me two small pots and a small stove. This is to show how my situation was then, but I refused to complain. Our tithes and offerings were not enough to pay the fees of a primary school pupil, yet I had to take the money to our district headquarters every month. Most of the journey I made then was either for church planting or revival programmes by trekking. At times, l walked five kilometers or more for church planting and revival programmes. Some of the greatest weapons of warfare of the marine witchcraft are isolation, poverty, lack of knowledge, sickness, and fear. When I began to think of my future, i got discouraged. Then a voice would be asking me: "Are you not going to marry and get children?" In addition, when I began to think in that direction, the enemy would be showing me my opportunities, the ones I had missed and the ones I could still embrace.

By 1990, I started getting discouraged. My prayer life went down, although I was the only person who understood what was happening. However, I kept everything to myself. My district pastor was also suffering, so I decided not to disturb him. I was therefore suffering in discouragement. All my mates were doing exploits in the cities, schools and their life's chosen jobs why I was caring Bible, preaching from place to place. There was no decent house to live in my family and others were making money in the cities, building houses and driving big cars. My life was messed up in shame, disgrace and reproach. I started praying for God to bless my immediate elder brother in America with money to come and build house. Looking at my condition at that time, I never believed I can ever feed myself not to talk of marriage or building a house, so I prayed that my brother would do. As I was praying, I saw in my dream, I was dressed up in a very nice suit that was very glorious. I saw many people following me, including my brother in USA with very dirty clothes. We headed to a very big bank that the workers were like angel. We stopped at a very big counter of the bank demarcating staffs and customers. My brother was at my immediate back with some other people. The bank staffs asked for my name and I told them. They started searching and found my name and they shouted for joy. They started shipping money in the counter before me but one strange thing happened, instead of giving me the money, they gave it to my brother at my back and I woke up. I kept fasting for God to bless my brother with money to come and build house. After a while, a message came from my village that my brother had returned from the United States of America and wanted to see me. I came home looking sick and tired. He gave me a box full of all manner of things – shoes, shirts, pairs of trousers, suits, "polo shirts," money and other things I needed. I later discovered that God could bless a person anywhere you are if you believe. Your unbelief and lack of knowledge can bless another person who may in turn give you less than one percent of what you labor for or nothing. I also learnt that some occultic people may exchange your destiny and while you suffer and labor, they make more gains through your suffering Acts 16:16, 18…

By the time, he was going back; we agreed that I should go back to Lagos first thing the following month i.e. January 1991. By December 1990, I had notified my district pastor who objected but when he saw my determination, he allowed me. Therefore, by January

1991, I was in Lagos waiting for my brother to send money to me for business. By the time he got back to the USA, he met problems in his office because of the Gulf War that was on then. In addition, while he was looking for another job, the American government placed an embargo on employment. It was then impossible for him to send money for me to set up a business as we agreed.

Moreover, because I did not want to go back into the ministry as a minister again, I decided to get money to set up a business. Nevertheless, all efforts failed. Every good door was closed against me while every bad ones (doors) was opened. In addition, all the demons I cast out in the village were waiting for me to enter. I understood very well the consequences of going into sin because my church then was very good at preaching against sin. We were always conscious of "righteousness and holiness without which no man shall see the Lord." There was no manner of abusive language that I knew I did not use against Satan.

Therefore, I decided that it would be better for me to die than commit sin willingly, which would hand me over to my archenemy – Satan and the Queen of Heaven. I remembered that at times, I would pray for hours, sing for hours, dance in my room for hours and use many hours to abuse Satan. For these reasons, I abhorred backsliding.

However, to some extent, my leaving the work of God was a manipulation from the marine powers to expose me to attack but it was a conscious sin that would then allow them to strike. One early morning, a relation of mine with whom I was staying, called me and introduced me to a boy who was selling radiators (419 Mercedes-Benz Lorries). I then went to the market for a "market survey" and discovered that the product was very scarce. The dealers who were my friends were very anxious to buy the product from me. When I left Idumota market for Ikeja, a thought came to me: to ask the young man how he came about the goods. Another thought was saying to me: "Just do the business and take your profit."

The amount I needed to set up a comfortable motor parts business at that time in Lagos was thirty thousand Naira only. Moreover, the profit I was to make within thirty minutes from the radiator "business" was exactly, thirty thousand Naira. I got confused. I started thinking that the young man in question must have stolen those radiators. I then called the young man and asked him how he got the radiators. He mentioned the company he was working for and said it was by "business." I quickly understood what he meant but I pretended not to have understood him.

Then upon further interrogations, he said rather impatiently."I said "By business" and you are still asking me how" Are you not a Nigerian? In Nigeria, a thief will not tell you that he is a thief. If he steals and wants to sell the stolen items to you, he will simply tell you that he got them by "business." Therefore, I knew what he was saying. I then told him that as a security guard in his company, he supposed to protect all the goods in his company. He said that is so but that everybody would like to do business whenever the opportunity came. He also told me that even the chief security guard was aware of that particular "business."

Then, I was a young vibrant and militant Christian, who has no diplomacy, calm approach or negotiation for evil acts. I told him that he was a thief. He then jumped out of the shop, went to my in-law and narrated all that I said to him. My in-law then said to the security man. "What he is saying is correct but I do not want to know how you got it. I am only interested in buying it from you whichever way you got it is not my concern." Immediately my in-law started talking like that, I left them and went to the house. In addition, the man was supposed to be a Christian.

Several times the enemy tried to destroy me through sin but the Lord always rescued me. On many occasions, the two girls in the house where we lived wanted to defile me. I only escaped by the grace of God. There was nothing that the marine powers did not use to make me fall into sin. Nevertheless, the Lord helped me and made me always conscious of my orientation – that sin should be avoided as one would avoid a viper. While I was in Lagos, waiting for the money from the USA, one of my fellow pastors and some members were seriously praying for me.

To be sincere, there was nothing I did not do to get money in a right way but all my efforts failed. From January to September 1991, things went rough for me, and all those who tried to help me. I tried to learn the art of printing but it was not possible for me to go into it. By the end of September, I started praying and asking God to have mercy on me. After praying for sometime, I got the lead to go back but I said that it would be better for me to start in Lagos. I tried but to no avail. In several ways, the Lord proved to me that my ministry in the village was yet to be completed.

At the time, I decided to go back, I asked my relation to give me the transport fare but he refused and said many things against my going back. One of the things he said which touched me was that I was confused. Truly, I was confused but I did not expect that statement from him because he was supposed to be a Christian. He refused to give me the transport money back to the village and he confiscated even the money I gave him to keep for me. I entered into the room and prayed: "God, if it is your will for me to go back, provide the means." After praying, I went to a location of Lagos called Oshodi to see one of my converts who was then a worker in the church.

As we were discussing, he told me that they would be traveling to my hometown the next day. I asked him if I could join them in their vehicle and he promptly told me that there would be a chance for me, as they would be going home in a car. Early in the morning the next day we started the journey and by evening we had arrived at my hometown. Immediately I returned, somebody told me that there was a problem in my former church and that the leadership in the district was going to discuss it that night. That evening, I met my district pastor, the other pastor who was my prayer partner as well as other pastors including the pastor who replaced me. At the end of the discussion the following morning, it was discovered that the marine powers had polluted the air with immorality.

The next day the district pastor asked me to go back to the church. That same month I left Lagos, the person that was to give me money from the USA got a job. If God calls you, nobody can help you to do any other thing in life. Many people have been disappointed because of my decision for the ministry. I have tried many things in life, and in all, I succeeded but lost my joy. In addition, of late, I found out that I could not do any other thing in life successfully. The greatest battle I have ever fought in life is the battle to escape the call of God. Nevertheless, I always failed. Who can battle with the Lord?

In November 1997, I was led to leave my exalted position as a district pastor in my former church and wait for the next instruction. On 22 December 1997, I was in Port Harcourt, where I fasted and prayed for about one month. Business opportunities opened up and during the heat of the scarcity of petroleum products in the country, a friend of mine who was working in an oil company registered me to be lifting petroleum products from the Port Harcourt refinery. It was not easy getting the license but with his influence as a manager, I was able to scale through all the hurdles without giving a bribe to anybody. I got my first and second allocations and made a profit that ran into hundreds of thousands of naira. I was happy and that was another opportunity for me to escape the call of God after about twelve years of being a pastor. I did not know that God wanted me to use the money to settle my immediate problems and get back into the ministry. As I was trying to get into business fully, my friend got another better job and I could not continue to lift the product again without getting involved in bribery. Again, pieces of advice started coming: "Do it, look at other Christians who do it." Moreover, truly, I saw leaders of different Pentecostal churches giving bribes to get their allocations but the spirit of God did not allow me to do that, moreover, my friend who got a better job somewhere else advised me to forget about the business since it would not help my Christian life. Jeremiah 44: 15-18 says:

Then shall it be for a man to burn: for he will take thereof, and warm himself; yea, he kindleth it, and baketh bread yea, he maketh a god, and worshippeth it he maketh it a graven image and falleth down thereto. He burneth part thereof in the fire; with part thereof he eateth flesh; he roasteth roast, and is satisfied; yea, he warmeth himself, and saith Aha, I am warm, I have seen the fire. And the residue thereof he maketh a god even his grave image: he falleth down unto it, and worshippeth it, and prayeth unto it, and saith. Deliver me, for thou art my god. They have not known nor understood: for he hath shut their eyes, that they cannot see, and their hearts, that they cannot understand.

The queen of heaven understands the battle very well. She finds it difficult to deal with anybody who is attached to God and who is staying where God wants him to stay. The first sign of the heavenly call is an intense, all-absorbing desire to do the work of God. It is bad to enter the ministry if you can help it. I tried to escape it but I could not. In addition, I want to say that if anybody is contented in his particular profession or trade, let him go his way; he is not called into the ministry. Somebody came to me for what he called "a combined ministry business" with ten million naira but I would not do such a thing because the ministry is not a business venture. Another person sent one million naira from Britain through somebody for what he also termed "combined business" with me, but I am not interested in such a thing because of evil conditions. The work of God must be done in a sincere way and to the glory of God. In 1996, I was posted to pastor a church in a marine-spirit dominated town. In addition, because I had decided not to be afraid of any evil power, I accepted the offer. One man of God in that town who I was told had challenged the occult kingdom of that town was disgraced out of that community by the spirit of immorality. He ran away from that town and the occultic people he had disturbed went with the police and arrested him. His house cleaner whom he impregnated and another member of his church – a woman who took the house cleaner for abortion as her mother – were all brought to the police station. It was a disgrace to the gospel.

One other "Reverend" minister of his church as well as the sectional leader was also afflicted with an incurable sickness that took his church a lot of money without success. The man was rushed out of the town; but before long, his wife and daughter were affected by the same horrible sickness. The last time I saw him in that town, he told me that twenty-one pins had come out of his body in addition to those of his wife and daughter. Many horrible things were happening in that town. I gathered all our five churches together with their pastors. Moreover, after preaching, I made an altar call for those who were willing to fast and pray three days and three nights. More than fifty-one people came out that Sunday morning. A team of our church evangelists was to come for a crusade the same week from the city. We then started fasting and praying in the village where the head demon in the town was located. All of us left our house for prayers in that village. I had never prayed or seen people pray the way we did that day. The baptism of the Holy Ghost was poured down like rain. People spoke in tongues for hours and prayer was easy for the three days and three nights. We started on the Monday of that week and rounded off on Thursday morning. On Friday morning, with high expectations and happiness for"a job well done," we were waiting for the evangelistic team from Onitsha. We waited to no avail and I had to preach very late to the crusade attendant.

They finally arrived about midnight after many hindrances on their way. The next day we were on the stage again with great expectations. Our members had gone out to tell people that it was going to be great. Therefore, people came in great numbers. Since that was a village, the evangelistic team decided to show films. The film they wanted to show refused to bring out any picture. They tried and tried but all was in vain. Each time the film started, the generator would go off immediately.

The crowd was laughing at us, while every one of us (Christians) was confused and surprised. We prayed all night, bound and loosed the best way we knew. The next day was Saturday. In addition, as the team of technicians we invited were working on the generator, the crowd gathered again. Some other generators were hired. It started working. A heavy rainfall descended without any previous sign and sent everyone running helter skelter. The next day, Sunday, the programme was held inside the church building. It was a big disappointment, and the leader of the team told me that they would come again but they never did. I was confused and could not understand how that kind of thing could happen after three days and three nights of prayers by more than fifty-one believers. The following morning, (Monday), they left for Onitsha.

However, the wicked marine power followed them and the team had an accident that claimed the life of one of the team members. In fact, many of them nearly died. The vehicle was badly damaged. It was a big loss but that incident helped me to understand the strength of the power of the marines in that community. I was ready to revenge. I knew that ordinary prayers would just provoke them and they could just clear the church, so I started preparing the members on how to fight a spiritual warfare in righteousness and faith. I told them the challenge ahead, and how it amounted to an insult for evil powers in that town to drink the blood of our brother.

All of us agreed to revenge. Everybody was angry against those powers in the town. We then started what we called relay prayer and fasting programme. Some people prayed for ten days and ten nights; some seven days and seven nights while some others had more or less number of days and nights to do their own prayers. The chain prayer was conducted in this manner: Group 1 started in the morning of the first day and prayed until the next morning but would not leave the church until Group 2 have come in and started their own prayers.

The chain-prayers lasted for fifty-six days and nights. In addition, within that period, many things happened.

One sister, Cecilia from Amachalla, who was chained in the house of a popular native doctor called Dr Onu, was healed of madness by our prayers. The young unmarried native doctor had a very big compound where people who came from all parts of the nation to consult him stayed. He was so popular that other native doctors envied him. They had tried to kill him many times but he always escaped their plans. Sometimes, he would disappear and at other times, he would just scatter them. In that town, he bewitched the people just like Simon did to the people of Samaria (Acts 8); like Bar-Jesus or Elymas the sorcerer bewitched his people and sought to turn away the deputy from Christ; and like Demetrius bewitched the people of Ephesus with a goddess called Diana. The native doctor in question was feared and respected almost like God. There were other terrible native doctors and herbalists but this one called "Doctor" was the greatest around them. About ninety-five percent of the people in that community of nineteen big villages were his "converts," i.e. they believed in him.

When we started our relay-prayer and fasting programme, fire was being sent to the houses and altars of those native doctors. By the middle of our bombardment with our prayers and fasting, the spiritual climate of that town became too hot. Confusion was seen everywhere. Many problems started in all the white garment churches. To my greatest surprise, people started leaving their groups to our church. One fateful day, I was told that "the great native doctor" was missing. It was unbelievable. For several weeks, his people and the entire town were in confusion. His corpse was later found in a river between that community and another town. On investigation, I learnt that other native doctors conspired and wrote a "letter charm" and sent it to him. They said that as soon as he received the letter, he quickly left his consulting room and all the tied people who were waiting for him. Moreover, without talking to anybody, he left the compound alone and dashed out into the waiting hands of some other native doctors who arrested him somewhere, and after manhandling him, tied a heavy load on his back and pushed him inside the river where he later died.

For though we walk in the flesh, we do not war after the flesh, we do not war after the flesh: for the weapons of our warfare are not carnal, but mighty through God to the pulling down of strongholds: casting down imaginations, and every high things that exalted itself against the knowledge of God, and bringing into captivity every thought to the obedience of Christ (II Cor. 10: 3-5).

As the prayer continued, and even after the prayer, violence increased among the heathen. After the death of "the great native doctor," his family and village were loosed to violence. On investigation, it was discovered that other native doctors were responsible. Therefore, the whole town nearly went into an inter-village war but the surrounding villages and towns collected all the native doctors in the village communities and handed them over. In addition, that was how the towns were spiritual and physically cleansed by the prayers of the saints –

using Egyptians against Egyptians. Within the same period, one huge snake – a very long snake - crawled to the most powerful shrine in the town in the presence of the elders and died there. The elders advised the young ones not to touch the snake – believing that it would soon move out. The snake lay in the centre of that shrine and decayed. Every night and day, our prayers were like thunder. Every morning, some people would come in front of the church to abuse us while others came to receive prayers.

The numerical strength of the church increased while members were also growing spiritually; people were being baptized with the Holy Ghost. There were frequent clashes between one group and another fighting and killing here and there. Nevertheless, all these things made others afraid, and many ran into the church. There were mysterious problems and no native doctors to run to, as the few left could no more perform. Therefore, in the prevailing circumstances, people were being saved. My wife was pregnant at that time, receiving attacks from these agents of darkness. I sent my wife to my hometown towards the ninth month of her pregnancy because the situation was too tense. The relay prayer and fasting programme lasted for fifty-six days and nights.

The programme ended on 22nd December, 1996, with testimonies. I left the town the same day to see my wife whose pregnancy had entered the eleventh month. Moreover, that was the only year I did not go for the December retreat in my previous church- a programme I had attended for thirteen previous years. I could not go because immediately I got home that day; my wife was delivered of male twins. The "war" was so much that my babies had to come out with their legs first (an abomination in my town). I named the first, Prayer because he was born out of prayers while the second son who died after four days of battle was named Praise. I love twins very much. So I prayed for a better replacement. And I asked God to invest all the good things in Praise into the life of Prayer. The Lord answered my prayers and on 30 April 2000, my wife gave birth to another set of twins – male and female – named Signs and Wonders respectively. The Lord is good.

On Tuesday 20th March 2001, one of our ministers told me that our church had its first Sunday fellowship in that town where marine churches were many. Four days later, precisely on 24th March, 2001 (a Saturday), I was told by another minister that the occultic house had been given to our church for fellowship though some people protested saying that after the first Sunday service, the gods of that town were not happy about the presence of the church. I told him that even if it was only that Sunday we were allowed, I was happy because thirteen years after a request, the Lord had then answered my prayers; and the occultic house was given for church service. By this time, the occultic society had crumbled to the glory of God. No prayer is a waste.

Today, Christianity has come to stay in that town. I have met many people from that town who are born again in truth and in spirit. One young man from that town came for deliverance two years ago when I was a deliverance minister at Enugu. He was mad and so sickly that the security guard in the church suspected that the man had AIDS and as a result, was too afraid to allow him to sleep in the church. I had to beg the security guard to allow the young man to sleep inside the church building. At the end of the deliverance, the young man came to his senses and came for counseling. As I was talking to him, he wanted to know my name and I told him. He then told me the name of his community and went ahead to let me now how he got mad. His mother happened to be one of the priestesses in one of the marine churches in the town. One day, the youths came home and destroyed his mother's altar. This young man said that all those who destroyed the altar began to have problems. Some lost their businesses while he became mad because of that. When he heard about deliverance, he then decided to come for deliverance. He underwent deliverance on two consecutive occasions before he came to his senses. After about two year, I saw him and he was testifying that he had gained admission into the Enugu State University of Science and Technology {ESUT}

To fight the queen of heaven, you must be sure of your:

1.   Repentance and fruits of repentance, e.g. transformation (Luke 15: 17-22, Matt. 3: 8-10, Luke 3: 8-14; Acts 26: 20; Matt. 21: 28-31; Jonah 3: 5-10). Repentance necessarily leads to a change of conduct because a change of mind must produce a change of character. Repentance is a change of mind-one that goes much deeper and involves a lot more than a mere change of opinion or creed. Repentance and transformation of life are inseparable. Repentance consists of radical change of mind about God, sin, self and the world. Previously, God was resisted, now He is accepted as our rightful Lord. Sin was a thing of

delight previously but now it is hated and mourned over. Repentance softens the hard soil of the soul and makes it receptive to the gospel seed.

2. **Faith in Christ (John 1:12-13; Acts 16: 30-34, John 3: 16-18).** To have faith in Christ is to put our complete trust in Him for forgiveness, peace and reconciliation with God. When you repent and believe in the Lord Jesus Christ, you are saved.

3. **Brokenness and righteousness at all times** (See Job 4:5-6, Isaiah 35: 8-10). Your repentance must produce the fruits of righteousness and new life. Any man or woman who continues in the old ways – using evil slangs, jokes, jest and evil conversations, dressing in the old worldly ways and practicing old business tricks, etc has not repented. Repentance brings reformation, righteousness and renewal. Those who remain cold and lukewarm in spiritual matters identify themselves with the impenitent world. Judgment is coming and all will be there. Those who do not have the righteousness required by God will not escape on that great Day of Judgment.

4. **Holy Ghost Baptism (Acts 2: 4)**

    Moreover, they were all filled with the Holy Ghost, and began to speak with other tongues, as the spirit gave them utterance.

Speaking in tongues is another weapon, which destroys the queen of heaven and Satan's government.

PRAYER SECTION

BREAKING EVIL MARRIAGES

1. Spiritual sexual abomination in my dream, disappear, in the name of Jesus.

2. Every authority of evil marriage in my life, be broken unto death, die, in the name of Jesus.

3. Every authority of satanic union in my dream, be nullified, in the name of Jesus.

4. Father Lord, commission me for marital success, in the name of Jesus.

5. O Lord, commission me for victory over spiritual sex manipulation, in the name of Jesus.

6. Every spiritual armed robber tormenting me in the dream sexually, I command you to die, in the name of Jesus.

7. I rain the fire of God on the spiritual strongman manipulating me in the dream, in the name of Jesus

8. I rain fire of God on spirit wife/husband disturbing my marriage, in the name of Jesus.

9. O Lord, let heavenly destruction come upon the remote control power used against my marriage, in the name of Jesus.

10. You domineering power of the spirit husband/wife in the dream, I dominate you, in the name of Jesus.

11. Evil effects of sexual relations in my dreams, be reversed, in the name of Jesus.

12. Every spiritual child from evil sexual dreams, die, in the name of Jesus.

13. Thou inordinate affections with the spirit husband/wife, be broken by fire, in the name of Jesus.

14. Every written document in support of spiritual marriage, catch fire and burn, in the name of Jesus.

15. Evil spiritual union with the spirit husband/wife, I renounce you, in the name of Jesus.

16. Thou destructive marriage in dream, be consumed by the fire of God, in the name of Jesus.

17. Any evil marriage certificate in the spirit realm, burn to ashes completely, in the name of Jesus.

18. I reject all evil possessions of spirit husband/wife in my life, in the name of Jesus.

19. I withdraw my reproductive organ deposited in the altar of spirit husband/wife, in the name of Jesus.

20. All evil material deposits in my body, come out and roast, in the name of Jesus.

21. Thou spiritual evil relatives, what are you waiting for? Die, in the name of Jesus.

22. All my activities in the spirit world negating my earthly marriage, die, in the name of Jesus.

23. All evil operations in the dream manipulating my body for evil, collapse and die, in the name of Jesus.

24. All evil hermaphrodites in my dream, somersault and die, in the name of Jesus.

25. Any strong man responsible for abnormal menstrual cycle via my dream, receive the judgment of God, in the name of Jesus.

26. O Lord, quench the power of polygamous spirit in my life, in the name of Jesus.

27. Thou spirit of intensive sexual thought in my heart, submit yourself, in the name of Jesus.

28. Thou spirit of uncontrollable sexual urge in my life, be paralyzed, in the name of Jesus.

29. I command the spirit husband/wife causing miscarriages in my life to enter into the dearth trap of God, in the name of Jesus.

30. Any satanic protection from evil spirit culminating in evil spiritual marriage in my dream, I nullify you, in the name of Jesus.

31. O Lord, deliver me from spiritual night raiders, in the name of Jesus.

32. Father Lord, command breakages upon covenants and evil linkages to spirit wife/husband in my life, in the name of Jesus.

33. O Lord, let every locust, caterpillar and palmerworm assigned to eat the marital blessings of my life be roasted by the fire of God, in the name of Jesus.

34. I paralyze every strong man attached to my marriage, in the name of Jesus.

35. Thou sun, moon and stars, act in my favor for God's sake, in the name or Jesus.

36. O Lord, command total deliverance upon my married life, in the name of Jesus.

37. O Lord, let the careful siege of the enemy over my life come to nothing, in the name of Jesus.

38. I release myself from the enchantments of the spirit personalities by the power of the Holy Spirit, in the name of Jesus.

39. Every marine enchantment over my earthly marriage, die, in the name of Jesus.

40. Any evil agreement of my ancestors with spirit beings against my marriage, die, in the name of Jesus.

41. Thou old evil relationship troubling my marital life, I break you, in the name of Jesus.

42. I command you spirit of oppression in my dream, die, in the name of Jesus.

43. Evil spiritual partner, divorce me now and die, in the name of Jesus.

44. My reproductive organs, receive total deliverance from every satanic oppression, in the name of Jesus.

45. O earth, consume every spiritual partner pursuing my life, in the name of Jesus.

46. I command the thunder of God to tear apart and consume every spirit wife/husband dominating my dream life, in the name of Jesus.

TOTAL FREEDOM FROM LEVIATHAN

1.   Lord, arise and crush every leviathan power targeting against my life, in the name of Jesus.

2.   I break and loose myself from every serpentine bondage, in the name of Jesus.

3.   Every witchcraft and serpent problems in my life, die, in the name of Jesus.

4.   Blood of Jesus, fight my battle now, in the name of Jesus.

5.   By the power in the words of God, I break the backbone of marine witchcraft, in the name of Jesus.

6.   Every friendly witch or wizards in my life, roast the name of Jesus.

7.   Every serpentine poison in any area of my life dry up and die, in the name of Jesus.

8.   O Lord, command deliverance upon my foundation, in the name of Jesus.

9.   Every serpent of affliction, die, in name of Jesus.

10. Anointing of leviathan upon my life, vanish, in the name of Jesus.

11. O Lord, with thy sore, great and strong sword, destroy every marine attack upon my life, in the name of Jesus.

12. Every spirit of pride in my life, roast, in the name of Jesus.

13. Every inherited marine bondage, loose your hold, by the blood of Jesus, in the name of Jesus.

14. Let all the curses in the bible pursue my stubborn pursuers, in the name of Jesus.

15. I overcome the dragon, by the blood of the lamb and the words of my testimony, in the name of Jesus.

16. Every negative power targeted against me, backfire, in the name of Jesus.

17. Holy Ghost, charge my prayer life, in the name of Jesus.

18. I refuse to pray amiss, in the name of Jesus.

19. Every serpent and scorpion of affliction in my life, die, in the name of Jesus.

20. Holy Ghost, open my spiritual eyes, in the name of Jesus.

21. Heavenly marine powers, release my virtues, in the name of Jesus.

22. Every satanic crocodile destroying in the garden of my life, die by thunder, in the name of Jesus.

23. I pull down the confidence of the leviathan over my life, in the name of Jesus.

24. Every strange fire of leviathan, quench, in the name of Jesus.

25. Every dragon of demotion in my life, I set you ablaze, in the name of Jesus.

26. Let divine fire and brimstone baptize my leviathan unto death, in the name of Jesus.

27. Let all marine spiritual animals (cat, dogs, snakes, crocodiles) paraded against me, be chained and returned to their senders, in the name of Jesus.

28. Host of heaven, fight my battle now, in the name of Jesus.

29. Let the fire of God boil all evil rivers harboring demons for my sake, in the name of Jesus.

30. O Lord, deliver me from the spirit of crocodiles, in the name of Jesus.

31. My cries, provoke angelic violence, in the name of Jesus.

32. I reject serpentine deceit, in the name of Jesus.

33. Holy Spirit, I need your divine assistance, in the name of Jesus.

34. I speak unto the palaces of the leviathan and of the seas and rivers, in the name of Jesus.

35. Every leviathan pollution in my foundation, receive the blood of Jesus, in the name of Jesus.

36.   I refuse and reject ancestral covenant with water spirits, in the name of Jesus.

VICTORY OVER MARINE WITCHCRAFT

1. I bind unrepentant witchcraft with fetters of iron and chains, in the name of Jesus.

2. Every witchcraft battle at the edge of my breakthrough, die by fire, in the name of Jesus.

3. Every witchcraft stronghold in my life, collapse by fire, in the name of Jesus.

4. I withdraw my destiny from my witchcraft altar, in the name of Jesus.

5. Any covenant or curse operating in my life from a witchcraft coven, be revoked by fire, in the name of Jesus.

6. Every dark meeting held against me; receive the thunder of God, in the name of Jesus.

7. Every inherited spiritual handicap because of witchcraft transfer, I reject you by fire, in the name of Jesus.

8. Every witchcraft deposit in my life, melt by fire, in the name of Jesus.

9. Every witchcraft resistance to my prayer, be broken, in the name of Jesus.

10. Let every afflicting fire in my life die, in the name of Jesus.

11. I cast out the spirit of evil inheritance in my life, in the name of Jesus.

12. Every obstacle on my way to progress because of evil rearrangement, scatter, in the name of Jesus.

13. I reject the agenda and plan of witchcraft in my life, in the name of Jesus.

14. I reject the assignment and weapons of the wicked against my life, in the name of Jesus.

15. Every witchcraft decision challenging my household, be disgraced by fire, in the name of Jesus.

16. I command spiritual divorce between me and every power of darkness, in the name of Jesus.

17. Every genetic tie polluted by witchcraft influence, I flush you out of my family, in the name of Jesus.

18. I revoke every evil law used against my life and family, in the name of Jesus.

19. Every bewitched department of my life, receive fire, in the name of Jesus.

20. Every root of evil desires in my life and family, be roasted by fire, in the name of Jesus.

21. Every instrument of unrighteousness in my household because of witchcraft influence, die, in the name of Jesus.

22. Every witchcraft pillow in my home, collapse by fire, in the name of Jesus.

23. Every witchcraft re-arrangement of my finance, I reject you now, in the name of Jesus.

24. I command every witchcraft pregnancy against my life to be aborted now, in the name of Jesus.

25. Every dirty hand in my progress, I cut you off, in the name of Jesus.

26. Any area of my life under satanic anointing, I neutralize you by fire, in the name of Jesus.

27. All evil associations summoned for my destruction, scatter, in the name of Jesus.

28. Every satanic reinforcement against my destiny, catch fire, in the name of Jesus.

29. Everything done against me and my ministry with witchcraft pad locks, be nullified by the blood of Jesus, in the name of Jesus.

30. Let every iron-like curse working against my ministry break by the blood of Jesus, in the name of Jesus.

31. Let every compromise to the satanic kingdom targeted to frustrate my ministry scatter, in the name of Jesus.

32. Every witchcraft power hanging on any evil forest affecting my ministry, catch fire, in the name of Jesus.

33. Every limitation placed on my ministry because of witchcraft influence, be dismantled, in the name of Jesus.

34. Any of my potentials buried in evil forest, I exhume you by fie, in the name of Jesus.

35. Every anti-prayer material deposited in my life, die, in the name of Jesus.

36. Every satanic attempt to downgrade my potential, I smash you in the wall of fire, in the name of Jesus.

37. O Lord, baptize me with the fire that will dry the fire of witchcraft in my life and ministry, in the name of Jesus.

38. Every witchcraft spy delegated against my progress, be blind, in the name of Jesus.

39. 'Doors of tragedy, fashioned by witchcraft in my ministry, shatter by fire, in the name of Jesus.

40. Thou gate of humiliation in my life, shatter by fire, in the name of Jesus.

41. Everything my ancestor has done to pollute my life, be dismantled by the blood of Jesus, in the name of Jesus.

42. Every power siphoning my blessings, die, in the name of Jesus.

43. I loose my mind and soul from the bondage of witches, in the name of Jesus.

44. Any marine witchcraft chain binding my hands and feet from progressing, be broken and shatter to pieces, in the name of Jesus.

45. Any arrow shot into my life from any witchcraft powers, come out and go back to your sender, in the name of Jesus.

46. Let every spiritual weapon of wickedness fashioned against my life be roasted by fire, in the name of Jesus.

47. Every witchcraft power introducing evil soul ties in my life, die, in the name of Jesus.

48. Every monitoring gadget, remote controlling my life, be destroyed by fire, in the name of Jesus.

49. Any witchcraft practice, targeted against my life, backfire, in the name of Jesus.

DELIVERANCE FROM INORDINATE AFFECTIONS

1. Blood of Jesus, purify my inner man, in the name of Jesus.

2. I break, reject and renounce any evil soul tie I have had with secret societies, in the name of Jesus.

3. Any power introducing me to evil relationships, summersault and die, in the name of Jesus.

4. Any man, woman or power gathering information to cage my mind, release me and die, in the name of Jesus.

5. Any music of destruction going on in my heart, die now, in the name of Jesus.

6. I enthrone Jesus in my heart and let every evil king against my life fall down and die, in the name of Jesus.

7. Every internal promoter of evil soul-tie, receive frustration, in the name of Jesus.

8. Any evil thing, programmed into my blood to control my life, come out and die now, in the name of Jesus.

9. I break out from every evil soul-tie I had with any person, in the name of Jesus.

10. Any satanic chain linking me to any evil relationship, break to pieces, in the name of Jesus.

11. O Lord, arise and collect my stolen portion from evil friends, in the name of Jesus.

12. Any satanic priest, tying my life with any unfriendly friend, die without mercy, in the name of Jesus.

13. I refuse to supply information that will cage my soul, in the name of Jesus.

14. Armies of heaven, release destruction weapons against the weapon of evil friends, in the name of Jesus.

15. O Lord, incubate me with your fire and let every occult bewitchment release my mind, in the name of Jesus.

16. Fire of God; destroy every satanic walkie-talkie supplying information to my enemy, in the name of Jesus.

17. O Lord, empower me to reign with Christ, in the name of Jesus.

18. Evil seed of any evil soul-tie, die and decay, in the name of Jesus.

19. I refuse to be defeated in this battle, in the name of Jesus.

20. Father Lord, sanctify me wholly from every evil pollution, in the name of Jesus.

21. Arrows of any evil soul tie, break and release me, in the name of Jesus.

22. You my life, come back from the evil journey of evil relationships, in the name of Jesus.

23. Any evil power boasting over my life, be disgraced by fire, in the name of Jesus.

24. I command all my pursuing unfriendly friends to turn back and flee, in the name of Jesus.

25. I paralyze every weapon of my enemy, in the name of Jesus.

26. I reject and refuse to collect evil gifts of bewitchment, in the name of Jesus.

27. Any evil power that has walked into my life, walk out by fire, in t he name of Jesus.

28. Any demon carrying evil reports against my desire, die by fire, in the name of Jesus.

29. Anything stolen from me by any evil friend, I capture you back by fire, in the name of Jesus.

30. I release fire against any kingdom challenging God in my life, in the name of Jesus.

31. I burn every evil written against my affection, in the name of Jesus.

32. I dismantle every siege of evil soul tie, in the name of Jesus.

33. By the anointing of the Holy Ghost, I break every yoke of evil soul-tie, in the name of Jesus.

34. Fire of deliverance, burn in my bone against evil relationship going on in my life, in the name of Jesus.

35. O Lord, disappoint the devices of evil soul ties, in the name of Jesus.

36. Peace of God, suppress every confusion organized in my heart, in the name of Jesus.

37. Any evil power taking the upper hand in my desire, die by fire, by force, in the name of Jesus.

38. I must be delivered, whether the enemy likes it or not, in the name Jesus.

39. Any power that has eaten deep to the detriment of my life, receive fire of God mingled with the blood of Jesus, in the name of Jesus.

40. I bring the oil of the Holy Ghost upon rusted nut of evil soul-tie and I command it to break, in the name of Jesus.

41. I break and renounce any evil soul tie I have had or may have had with:

  ➢ Social organizations

  ➢ Religious leaders

  ➢ Past or present friends

  ➢ Clubs

  ➢ Close friends

  ➢ Engagements

- ➢ Cults
- ➢ Preachers
- ➢ Organizations
- ➢ Family members
- ➢ Husbands
- ➢ Acquaintances
- ➢ Wives,

  in the name of Jesus.

42. Every inherited evil soul tie, break and release me, in the name of Jesus.

43. I smash and destroy any wicked law ruling over my life, in the name of Jesus.

44. Any satanic filling station supplying fuel to evil friends to keep me under perpetual bondage, catch fire and burn, in the name of Jesus.

45. O God, arise and contend with every enemy of my spiritual growth, in the name of Jesus.

46. Any reporting demon following me from any evil relationship, die, by thunder, in the name of Jesus.

47. Divine immunity against evil soul ties; possess my life, in the name of Jesus.

48. You my life, become fire to every unfriendly friend, in the name of Jesus.

49. Anointing and glory of God, come upon my life now, in the name of Jesus.

50. Begin to thank God for He has answered your prayers, in the name of Jesus.

PULLING DOWN SATANIC SATELLITES

1. Any evil thing programmed into the sun, the moon and the stars against my life, be dismantled, in Jesus' name.

2. I speak unto the stars, the sun and the moon to favor me, in the name of Jesus.

3. Every satanic satellite mounted against my destiny; catch fire, in the name of Jesus.

4. I bring the blood of Jesus against any satanic barrier, mounted against me in the heavenlies, in Jesus' name.

5. Every satanic computer targeted against me, scatter, in the name of Jesus.

6. Any satanic satellite searching for my star, be dismantled, in Jesus' name.

7. I terminate every evil agreement between my enemies in the heavenlies, in Jesus' name

8. Every consultation of demons against me, die in Jesus' name.

9. I declare to the heavenlies that I am married to Jesus, in Jesus' name.

10. Any witchcraft-meeting going on in the heavenlies for my sake, scatter by thunder, in Jesus' name.

11. O Lord, water me from the water of heaven, in Jesus' name.

12. I conceal the secret of my life from the knowledge of the spiritual armed robbers, in Jesus' name.

13. All evil accusations piled up against me in the heavenly computer, receive divine explosion, in Jesus' name.

14. Let the power that raised Jesus from the dead break my yoke now, in Jesus' name.

15. Any heavenly monitor, checking the affairs of my life, roast, in Jesus' name.

16. Anything drawing powers against me from the heavenlies, fall down and die, in Jesus' name.

17. O Lord, upgrade my power, in Jesus' name.

18. Satanic anchor, roast, in Jesus' name.

19. Heavenly mounted witchcraft, scatter, in Jesus' name.

20. O God, arise, let every witchcraft plantation scatter, in the name of Jesus.

21. My destiny, escape from every prison, in the name of Jesus.

22. Anointing for open heavens, come upon me, in the name of Jesus.

23. I retrieve all my property dedicated to the sun, the moon, the stars and the elements by the power of darkness, in the name of Jesus.

24. You heavenlies, refuse to give reply to any satanic programming against my life, in the name of Jesus.

25. I dismantle every satanic calendar, in the name of Jesus.

26. Every evil handwriting, programmed by satanic agents into the heavenlies against my life, be wiped off, in the name of Jesus.

27. I retrench and frustrate satanic priests ministering enchantment into the sun, the moon and the stars, in the name of Jesus.

28. Holy Ghost, make me invisible for satanic satellites, in the name of Jesus.

29. I decree that all the elements will cooperate with me this year, in the name of Jesus.

30. I decree that the elemental forces will refuse to cooperate with my enemies this year, in the name of Jesus.

31. I speak unto the sun, the moon and the stars; you shall not smite my family and me this year, in the name of Jesus.

32. I pull down every negative planning to operate against my life this year, in the name of Jesus.

33. I confess that this is the year the Lord has made, I will rejoice and be glad in it, in the name of Jesus.

34. I shall possess the gate of my enemies this year, in the name of Jesus.

35. The Lord shall anoint me with the oil of gladness above my fellows this year, in the name of Jesus.

36. Let every satanic checkpoint mounted against me in the heavenlies be dismantled, in the name of Jesus.

37. Every evil altar prepared against my breakthrough in the heavenlies, be roasted by fire, in Jesus' name.

38. Every satanic television mounted in the water for my sake, break to pieces, in Jesus' name.

39. I command the careful siege of the enemy against my life to be dismantled, in the name of Jesus.

40. I send lightning, thunder, fire and sulphur from the third heaven against the evil queen in the heavenlies militating against my life, in Jesus' name.

41. I puncture every witchcraft's eyes, monitoring my destiny, in the name off Jesus.

42. I take divine insurance against all forms of accident and tragedy, in the name of Jesus.

43. Every satanic agent, capturing my prayers, be dismantled, in the name of Jesus.

44. Let the host of heaven wage war against the queen of heaven, queen of the cost and the leviathan power for my sake, in the name of Jesus.

45. Satanic operators, burning night candles for my sake, die, in the name of Jesus.

46. I refuse to be summoned in the occultic mirrors, in the name of Jesus.

47. Every satanic meeting in the Venus to summon my spirit, be frustrated by the stones of fire, in Jesus' name.

48. Let every scientific network organized against my life and family develop a fault, in Jesus' name.

49. Holy Spirit, release your wisdom upon my life, in the name of Jesus.

50. Any personality praying naked to the elements against me, be replaced on my behalf, in Jesus' name.

51. My name shall destroy every satanic satellite, in the name of Jesus.

52. Every source of power to my enemies, be switched off now, in Jesus' name.

53. I shake off every satanic magnet programmed into my life, in the name of Jesus.

54. I carry the warfare to the gate of the enemy, in the name of Jesus.

55. Every occultic man drawing powers from the sun to harm my life, be electrocuted now, in the name of Jesus.

56. Every negative power programming evil against my stall, fall down and die, in Jesus' name.

57. I recover all my virtues dedicated to the elements, in the name of Jesus.

58. Every satanic drier mounted in the heavenlies to dry up the waters of my life, turn against your owner, in Jesus' name.

59. Let the heavens and the elements declare the glory of God over my life, in the name of Jesus.

60. O Lord, reveal deeper things about the heavenlies for me, in Jesus' name.

61. I paralyze every satanic sophistication against me, in the name of Jesus.

62. The queen of heaven must regret coming in contact with me, in Jesus' name.

63. Where is the lord God of Elijah? Answer me now, in Jesus' name.

64. Blood of Jesus, fight my battle now, in Jesus' name.

65. Anything in my life making my life accessible to the powers of the heavenlies, come out now, in the name of Jesus.

66. I will make it, in Jesus' name.

67. Blood of Jesus, visit every legal ground of the queen of heaven over my life, in Jesus' name.

68. That angel that rolled away the tomb of Jesus, turn against every dark power targeted against me, in Jesus' name.

69. O Lord, mount me above satanic manipulation, in Jesus' name.

70. I release thunder and brimstone upon every satanic headquarters in the heavenlies, in Jesus' name.

71. O Lord, give me a spiritual name that the enemy cannot know, in the name of Jesus.

72. I command my name to disappear from every file of the queen of the coast, in Jesus' name.

73. I command my name to vanish from the satanic computer of the queen of heaven, in the name of Jesus.

74. Lord Jesus, fight for me until I overcome all my enemies, in Jesus' name.

75. Every satanic brain behind my problems, scatter in madness, in Jesus' name.

76. Holy Ghost, bully Satan for my sake, in Jesus' name.

77. O God of Joshua, give me the same power you gave to Joshua over the heavenlies, in Jesus' name.

78. Every heavenly witchcraft bird giving information about me, die by thunder, in Jesus' name.

79. Let my prayers become stones that will raise down every gadget mounted against my destiny in the heavenlies, in Jesus' name.

80. By the power given to me as a Son of God in John 1: 12, I paralyze every power from the heavenlies, in Jesus' name.

81. In the presence of the powers asking for my God, O God, arise and show them, in the name of Jesus.

82. I am seated in the heavenlies with Jesus far above all other principalities; therefore any satellites looking for me is wasting time, in Jesus' Name.

83. As the wind comes and goes without direction, so shall my spirit be, satanic satellites cannot locate my moves, in Jesus' name.

84. You the power operating between 12pm and 3am, my life is not your candidate, in Jesus' name

85. I am hidden in Christ, Christ in God, how can satanic satellites see my life? In Jesus' name.

86. Jehovah Jire, laugh my enemies to scorn, in Jesus' name.

87. Incantations, spells, divinations and bewitchment, come under my feet now, in Jesus' name.

88. Where is that spirit that raised Jesus from the dead? Resurrect any department of my life, killed by satanic programmes, in Jesus' name.

89. I refuse to be ignorant of the wicked heavenly witchcraft mechanisms, in the name of Jesus.

90. I shall posses my possessions, in Jesus' name.

91. By the power that dries the red sea, O Lord, answer my prayers, in Jesus' name.

92. Every satanic consultant working on my destiny, bow to the name of Jesus, in the name of Jesus.

93. Anyone who accepted witchcraft in order to disgrace my life, be disgraced, in Jesus' name.

94. By the power that disgraced Goliath, O Lord, answer my prayers, in the name of Jesus.

95. By all the powers by which you are known to be God, O Lord, answer my prayers, in Jesus' name.

96. Thank you Jesus for the queen of heaven and her agents are crying for my sake, in Jesus' name.

97. O God of vengeance, I thank you, in Jesus' name.

98. The God that created both the visible and invisible, thank you for answering my prayers, in Jesus' name.

PRAYER AGAINST SPIRITUAL CHILDREN

1. Every spiritual child attached to my life, I bind and cast you out, in the name of Jesus.

2. I refuse to be established by demonic children, in the name of Jesus.

3. I destroy the power of any demonic child in my life, in the name of Jesus.

4. Every link between any spiritual child and me, be broken now, in the name of Jesus.

5. Let all spirit children attached to my life be electrocuted, in the name of Jesus.

6. Any demonic child claiming me as their mother/father, die, in the name of Jesus.

7. Blood of Jesus, silence all spiritual children crying against me, in Jesus' name.

8. I bring the blood of the Lord over every spiritual child now, in Jesus' name.

9. I refuse and reject the ancestral covenant with any spiritual child, in Jesus' name.

10. I arrest you spiritual children and I command you to die, in Jesus' name.

11. I break the power of spirit children over every department of my life, in the name of Jesus.

12. Every spirit child in my life, gather yourselves together, collapse and die, in Jesus' name.

13. Lion of Judah, eat up every spirit child attached to my life, in the name of Jesus.

14. Every masquerading spiritual child working against me, summersault and die, in the name of Jesus.

15. I destroy the power of spiritual children in my life, in the name of Jesus.

16. O Lord, let your arrow be strong and pierce unto the hearts of my spirit children, in Jesus' name.

17. I plead the blood of Jesus against every spiritual child, in the name of Jesus.

18. All you spiritual children affecting my life, be chained unto death, in the name of Jesus.

19. Any spirit child drawing me away from God, die, in Jesus' name.

20. You the spirit children in my life, enter inside the dustbin of fire now, in the name of Jesus.

PRAYERS AGAINST INCURABLE SICKNESSES

1. Blood of Jesus, flush away particles of arthritis from my life, in the name of Jesus.

2. You spirit of arthritis, loose your hold and depart, in the name of Jesus.

3. I drink the blood of Jesus and I expel every spirit of asthma through my breath, in the name of Jesus.

4. You the whirlwind of God, blow away every wind of diabetes in my life, in Jesus' name.

5. Blood of Jesus, speak disappearance unto my asthma, in the name of Jesus.

6. Holy Ghost fire, destroy every stubborn agent of strokes in my life, in the name of Jesus.

7. You the agent of strokes working against my life, disappear, in the name of Jesus.

8. You the spirit behind this diabetes, come out with all your roots, in the name of Jesus.

9. Holy Ghost fire, burn away every asthma in my life, in the name of Jesus.

10. Father Lord, let your power move away every mountain of arthritis in my life, in the name of Jesus.

11. Any man, woman or power battling my health, receive the fire of God, in the name of Jesus.

12. O spirit of epilepsy, hear the word of the Lord, I command you, die, in the name of Jesus.

13. Every bondages of epilepsy, come out with all your roots, in the name of Jesus.

14. You the spirit of convulsion, I come against you, die, in the name of Jesus.

15. I rebuke every refuge of cancer in my life, in the name of Jesus.

16. O Lord, according to thy word, heal me and I shall be healed, in the name of Jesus.

17. O Lord, according to thy word, deliver me and I shall be delivered, in the name of Jesus.

18. I destroy the grip and operation of HIV and Ebola in my life, in the name of Jesus.

19. O power in the stripes of Jesus, destroy the spirit of epilepsy in me, in the name of Jesus.

20. Fire of God, locate and destroy the power behind the cancer in my life, in the name of Jesus.

21. I command every agent of strokes in my blood and body organs to die, in the name of Jesus.

22. I hold the blood of Jesus against the spirit of cancer; you must die, in the name of Jesus.

23. O Lord, let your whirlwind blow every wind of HIV and Ebola away from me, in the name of Jesus.

24. I minister death unto the spirit of HIV and Ebola in my life, in the name of Jesus.

25. I annul every engagement with the spirit of HIV and Ebola, in the name of Jesus.

26. I command every deposit of HIV in my life to be melted away by the fire of the Holy Ghost, in the name of Jesus.

27. Every plantation of HIV and Ebola in my life, die, in the name of Jesus.

28. I break the backbone of epilepsy working against my life, in the name of Jesus.

29. I come against every power in heaven on earth and under the earth that will stand as a mountain against my healing, in the name of Jesus.

30. I set myself free 3 times from the spirit of diabetes and Ebola, in the name of Jesus.

31. I paralyze every power behind the extension and expansion of my problems, in the name of Jesus

32. You the agent of health destruction in my family, fall down and die, in the name of Jesus.

33. You the power blocking the possibility into my problem, fall down and die, in the name of Jesus.

34. O Lord, let every deeply entrenched situation in my life dry from the root now, in the name of Jesus.

35. Blood of Jesus, speak deliverance to any bondage situation in my life, in the name of Jesus.

36. I command death upon you stubborn sickness in my life, in the name of Jesus.

37. You the spirit standing against my perfect healing, fall and die, in the name of Jesus.

38. I decree and declare death upon any spirit working against my health, in the name of Jesus.

39. You the agent of sickness, bringing stubbornness to my situation, disappear, in the name of Jesus.

40. O Lord, arise and let every power of stubborn sickness in me scatter, in the name of Jesus.

41. You the rod of sickness, loose your hold, in the name of Jesus.

42. O Rock of Ages, grind every infirmity in me to powder, in the name of Jesus.

43. O Lord, let my stubborn situation be swallowed up by your fire, in the name of Jesus.

44. You the spirit of sickness troubling my life, be terminated, in the name of Jesus.

45. I command all unfriendly helpers responsible to my condition to die, in the name of Jesus.

46. O Lord, arise and bring a final solution to every stubborn problem in my life, in the name of Jesus.

47. Every stubborn sickness pattern for my life, break, in the name of Jesus.

48. O Lord, let every power tying me down to sickness fall down and die, in the name of Jesus.

49. O Lord, uproot the cause of any sickness in my life, in the name of Jesus.

50. Let the agents of impossibility working against my healing be paralyzed, in the name of Jesus.

51. I reject partial or temporary healing; I embrace complete healing, in the name of Jesus.

52. I paralyze every power delaying my healing, in the name of Jesus.

53. You the strong man in charge of the sickness in my life, die, in the name of Jesus.

54. You the problem in my life, I arrest you from the root, in the name of Jesus.

55. I release the anger of God upon the condition of my life, in the name of Jesus.

56. You the power in charge of my sickness, drink the water of affliction, in the name of Jesus.

57. Every stronghold of sickness in me, I shatter you to pieces, in the name of Jesus.

58. O Lord, let the concrete constructed by the enemy to stop the germination of my healing be broken to pieces, in the name of Jesus.

59. You the power of sickness in my life, I march upon you and cross over you, in the name of Jesus.

60. You the sickness troubling my body, die, in the name of Jesus.

61. O Lord, let any power that would want to bring the sickness back summersault and die, in the name of Jesus.

62. I grab every stubborn problem in my life and smash it against the rock of my salvation, in the name of Jesus.'

63. Blood of Jesus, poison the root of my problems, in the name of Jesus.

64. O Lord, let every thing the enemy has said is impossible in my life be possible, in the name of Jesus.

65. Let the blood of Jesus speak disappearance unto every infirmity in my life, in the name of Jesus.

66. You the knee of infirmity and virus in my life, bow, in the name of Jesus.

67. I command death upon you sickness troubling my life, in the name of Jesus.

68. O Lord, let every stubborn problem seed in my life be uprooted by fire, in the name of Jesus.

69. You the power that re-arranges sickness in my life, die, in the name of Jesus.

70.   O heavenly doctor, carry out a surgical operation in my life, in the name of Jesus.

71.   You the deeply rooted problem in my life, be uprooted by fire, in the name of Jesus.

72.   Divine health; come upon me, in the name of Jesus.

73.   Father Lord, let everything working against my health be destroyed by your life, in the name of Jesus.

74.   Heavenly Father, transfer me from sickness to divine health, in the name of Jesus.

75.   O thou God of health, heal me now, in the name of Jesus.

76.   You the sickness troubling my body, I hold the blood of Jesus against you, in the name of Jesus.

77.   I declare every germ of infirmity in my body dead, in the name of Jesus.

78.   O Lord, let every cooperation with sickness in my body consciously or unconsciously, be broken, in the name of Jesus.

79.   I paralyze every stubborn sickness demon troubling my soul with the blood of Jesus, in the name of Jesus.

80.   I stand upon the word of God and declare myself healed, in the name of Jesus.

81. Every staying power of the problems in my life, die, in the name of Jesus.

82. You the demon of terminal disease, I burn you today, in the name of Jesus.

83. Every stubborn agent of disease in my body, receive the fire of God, in the name of Jesus.

84. I boil out of my system every infirmity and virus with Holy Ghost Fire, in t he name of Jesus.

85. (Lay your hands on your head and stomach and pray thus) Every problem in my body, that place is not your house; depart, in the name of Jesus.

86. O Lord, let every power protecting the sickness in my life die, in the name of Jesus.

87. You the source of sickness, death in my family, dry up, in the name of Jesus.

88. I declare the exit of every power bringing problems into my life, in the name of Jesus.

89. I break every vicious cycle of problems in my life, in the name of Jesus.

90. O Lord, send your heavenly surgeons to perform a surgical operation where necessary in my life, in the name of Jesus.

91. Lord Jesus, as has been done to Hezekiah, remove the garment of sickness from me, in the name of Jesus.

92. You the power re-arranging problems in my life, fall and die, in the name of Jesus.

93. Lord Jesus, let your final solution be brought to my stubborn situation, in the name of Jesus.

94. O Lord, let the day of my enemy over my health be turned to sorrow, in the name of Jesus.

95. You the Goliath of infirmity in my body, pack your loads and move out, in the name of Jesus.

96. O Lord, by your wonderful name, I command the spirit of the sickness of fibroid to disappear, in the name of Jesus.

97. I come against you stubborn cough, by the fire of the Holy Ghost, water and blood that was shed on the cross of Calvary, die now, in the name of Jesus.

98. Let the electrifying power of God almighty electrocute every power behind my infirmity, in the name of Jesus.

99. By the power that is in the blood of Jesus, i break my infirmity and destroy my diseases and declare myself healed, in the name of Jesus.

100. You the seed of infirmity in my life, I dry you up, in the name of Jesus.

PRAYER POINTS

1. Any covenant with the queen of heaven and other marine powers working against my life, break, in the name of Jesus.

2. Every evil pillar holding the foundation of the queen of heaven in my life, collapse by fire, in the name of Jesus.

3. Any man, woman or power re-building the foundation of the queen of heaven in my life, be frustrated by fire, in the name of Jesus.

4. Any marine witchcraft practiced under the water to attack my life, fail woefully, in the name of Jesus.

5. You my life, escape from every marine coven now, in the name of Jesus.

6. Every fear in my life from the marine kingdom, die, in the name of Jesus.

7. Any giant of darkness, monitoring my life from the marine kingdom, what are you waiting for? Fall down and die, in the mighty name of Jesus.

DELIVERANCE FROM THE QUEEN OF HEAVEN

1. Any covenant with the queen of heaven from my place of birth, break and release me, in the name of Jesus.

2. Any power facing the sun, moon or stars against me, die, in the name of Jesus.

3. Any water in my village manipulating my life, receive fire, in the name of Jesus.

4. Any invisible marine rings, chains and bangles, hiding inside me, be roasted by fire, in the name of Jesus.

5. Every marine prison, keeping me in bondage, release me and collapse, in the name of Jesus.

6. Every altar raised against my destiny by the queen of heaven, die, in the name of Jesus.

7. Every plantation in my life by the queen of heaven, come out and die, in the name of Jesus.

8. I take away my marriage from the hands of the queen of heaven, in the name of Jesus.

9. Let the voice of the blood of Jesus destroy every decree of the queen of heaven in my life, in the name of Jesus.

10. I receive power to destroy the throne of the queen of heaven in my life, in the name of Jesus.

11. Every midnight enchantment against me, die, in the name of Jesus.

12. Any crocodile in the water of my life, die, in the name of Jesus.

13. Let the occultic altar raised against me be uprooted by force, in the name of Jesus.

14. Any thing programmed into the heavens against me, I pull you down by force, in the name of Jesus.

15. My divine life partner, appear by fire, in the name of Jesus.

16. Every invitation given to Satan and the queen of heaven into my life, I withdraw you by fire, in the name of Jesus.

17. Every hold of the enemy in my life, scatter by thunder, in the name of Jesus.

18. Queen of heaven, die in my business/profession, in the name of Jesus.

19. Any evil mark that identifies me with the queen of heaven, he roasted by fire, in the name of Jesus.

20. Every problem in my life from the queen of heaven, gather yourself together and die, in the name of Jesus.

FREEDOM FROM WORLDLY SPIRITS

1. Worldliness in my family, what are you waiting for? Die by fire, in the name of Jesus.

2. My life, reject worldliness by fire, in the name of Jesus.

3. Any department of my life embracing worldliness, receive deliverance by fire, in the name of Jesus.

4. Every worldly spirit pursuing me from my place of birth, fall down and die, in the name of Jesus

5. Every foundation of worldliness in my life, collapse by fire, in the name of Jesus.

6. Spirit of worldliness, destroying people in this environment, somersault and die, in the name of Jesus.

7. Any power in this world, pulling me away from Christ, die, in the name of Jesus.

8. You the strongman, discouraging Christianity in the place of my birth, drink acid and die, in the name of Jesus.

9. Persecution, you will not take away my crown, in the name of Jesus.

10. Any fire of persecution, burning in my life, quench, in the name of Jesus.

11. Every arrow of discouragement and persecution fired into my Christian life, come out by fire, in the name of Jesus.

QUEEN OF HEAVEN, DIE!

1. Queen of heaven, sitting on my marriage, die, in the name of Jesus.

2. Queen of heaven, sitting upon my ministry, die, in the name of Jesus.

3. Queen of heaven, sitting upon my life, die, in the name of Jesus.

4. Any property of the queen of heaven inside my womb, come out by fire, in the name of Jesus.

5. Any problem I inherited from the throne of the queen of heaven, die, in the name of Jesus.

SPIRIT HUSBAND, WIFE, CONCUBINE AND CHILDREN

1. My spirit wife/husband, concubine and children, die, in the name of Jesus.

2. Any marriage certificate linking me to evil marriage, be roasted by fire, in the name of Jesus.

3. Any invisible marine spirit rings, bangles and chains in my life, I destroy you by fire, in the name of Jesus.

4. Every defeat I have suffered in a dream from spiritual armed robbers, be converted to victory, in the name of Jesus.

5. You my spiritual rapist, what are you waiting for? Fall down and die, in the name of Jesus.

DELIVERANCE FROM EVIL SOUL TIES

1. Every Delilah and Jezebel in my life, die without mercy, in the name of Jesus.

2. Any power that is tying my soul with an evil chain, release me and die, in the name of Jesus.

3. Any man, woman or power controlling me in an evil way, fall down and die, in the name of Jesus.

4. Any tree of evil desires growing inside me, be uprooted by fire, in the name of Jesus.

5. Blood of Jesus, repurchase me from every evil soul tie, in the name of Jesus.

6. Any pillar of the queen of heaven holding sin in my life, collapse by thunder, in the name of Jesus.

7. I shake every sin cleaving into my foundation, in the name of Jesus.

REFERENCES

Olukoya D. K. *Smite the Enemy and He will flee* Gwenshaw *Redeeming the Land.*

Author's Lecture *notes on Church History.*

Author's *Bible Study notes*

Thank You So Much

Beloved, I hope you enjoyed this book as much as I believe God has touched your heart today. I cannot thank you enough for your continued support for this prayer ministry.

I appreciate you so much for spending time to read this wonderful prayer book, and if you have an extra second, I would love to hear what you think about this book.

Please, do share your testimonies with me by sending an email to me at pastor@prayermadueke.com, also in facebook at www.facebook.com/prayer.madueke. I invite you to my website at www.prayermadueke.com to view many other books I have written on various issues of life, especially on marriage, family, sexual problems and money.

I will be delighted to partner with you also in organized crusades, ceremonies, marriages and marriage seminars, special events, church ministration and fellowship for the advancement of God's kingdom here on earth.

Thank you again, and I wish you nothing less than success in life.

God bless you.

Prayer M. Madueke

BOOKS BY PRAYER M. MADUEKE

- *21/40 Nights Of Decrees And Your Enemies Will Surrender*
- *Tears In Prison*
- *Prayers For Marriage And Family*
- *Prayers For Academic Success*
- *Organized Student In A Disorganized School*
- *Alone With God - Prayers For Finance*
- *Prayer Riots To Overthrow Divorce*
- *Prayers To Get Married Happily*
- *SPECIAL PRAYERS IN HIS PRESENCE*
- *Prayers For Good Health*
- *Prayer Retreat*
- *Prayers For Children And Youths*
- *35 Special Dangerous Decrees*
- *Youths, May I Have Your Attention Please?*
- *Alone With God - Prayers For Successful Career*
- *Welcome To Campus*
- *Prayers To Keep Your Marriage Out Of Troubles*
- *Prayers For Conception And Power To Retain*
- *Prayers For Nation Building*
- *Alone With God (Complete Version)*
- *General Prayers For Nation Building*
- *Prayers Against Satanic Oppression*
- *Prayers For A Successful Career*
- *Prayers For Deliverance*

- *Prayers For Financial Breakthrough*
- *Prayers For Overcoming Attitude Problems*
- *Contemporary Politicians' Prayers For Nation Building*
- *Veteran Politicians' Prayers For Nation Building*
- *Prayers To Marry Without Delay*
- *Prayers For Marriages In Distress*
- *Prayers To Prevent Separation Of Couples*
- *Prayers For Restoration Of Peace In Marriage*
- *Prayers To Triumph Over Divorce*
- *Prayers To Heal Broken Relationship*
- *Prayers To Pray During Courtship*
- *Prayers For Your Wedding*
- *Prayers To Pray During Honeymoon*
- *Prayers For Newly Married Couple*
- *Prayers To Experience Love In Your Marriage*
- *Prayers For Fertility In Your Marriage*
- *Prayers To Conceive And Bear Children*
- *Prayers To Preserve Your Marriage*
- *Prayers For Pregnant Women*
- *Prayers To Retain Your Pregnancy*
- *Prayers To Overcome Miscarriage*
- *Prayers To End A Prolonged Pregnancy*
- *Prayers To Deliver Your Child Safely*
- *Prayers To Raise Godly Children*
- *Prayers To Overcome An Evil Habit*
- *Prayers For Your Children's Deliverance*
- *Prayers To Live An Excellent Life*

- *Prayers For College And University Students*
- *Prayers For Success In Examination*
- *Prayers For An Excellent Job*
- *Prayers For A Job Interview*
- *Prayers To Progress In Your Career*
- *Prayers For Healthy Living And Long Life*
- *Prayers To Live And End Your Life Well*
- *Prayers For Breakthrough In Your Business*
- *Prayers Against All Manner Of Sickness And Disease*
- *Prayers For A Happy Married Life*
- *Prayers To Buy A Home And Settle Down*
- *Prayers To Receive Financial Miracles*
- *Prayers For Christmas*
- *Prayers For Widows And Orphans*
- *Prayers Against Premature Death*
- *Prayers For Sound Sleep And Rest*
- *40 Prayer Giants*
- *More Kingdoms To Conquer*
- *Prayer Campaign For Nigeria*
- *Fall And Rise Of The Igbo Nation*
- *Because You Are Living Abroad*
- *Americans, May I Have Your Attention Please!*
- *Community Liberation And Solemn Assembly*
- *The First Deliverance*

CONTACTS

AFRICA
#1 Babatunde close,
Off Olaitan Street, Surulere
Lagos, Nigeria
+234 803 353 0599
pastor@prayermadueke.com,

Plot 1791, No. 3 Ijero Close,
Flat 2, Area 1,
Garki 1 - FCT, Abuja

IRELAND
Ps Emmanuel Oko
#84 Thornfield Square
Cloudalkin D22
Ireland
Tel: +353 872 820 909, +353 872 977 422
aghaoko2003@yahoo.com

EUROPE/SCHENGEN
Collins Kwame
#46 Felton Road
Barking
Essex IG11 7XZ GB
Tel: +44 208 507 8083, +44 787 703 2386, +44 780 703 6916
aghaoko2003@yahoo.com